PAUL MORGAN

Rugby World Cup 2007

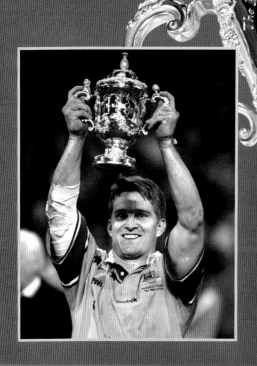

PaRragon

Bath · New York · Singapore · Hong Kong · Cologne · Delhi · Melbourne

E N T S

INTROD
the webb ellis cup

Rugby, like many sports, evolved over the centuries and has its heritage in the ball games that were played through the 18th and early 19th centuries. The game of rugby union almost certainly did not kick off for the first time with a young man called William Webb Ellis picking up the ball and running with it. That incredible story – which only surfaced after his death in 1872 – is best regarded as apocryphal, but Webb Ellis and his contemporaries at Rugby School were crucial in the establishment of the sport.

Historians believe that rugby developed out of one of the many sports, such as Camp-Ball and the Eton Wall game, played at England's public schools and, in particular, Rugby School in the early to mid-19th century. There are stories of senior boys at Rugby School meeting in the evening to review the games and suggest amendments for the following day's contests. The first set of rules – which would be unrecognisable from today's rugby union – surfaced around 1845 and it was these that those senior boys adjusted.

Jonny Wilkinson must be delighted he was not around at that time, as those early rules sound crazy today. They included the tactic of hacking, which allowed one player to kick another in the shins. The 2003 World Cup Final might have had a completely different ending had the Wallabies been able to kick Wilkinson in the shins! "Hacking was permitted in those rules," reported *The Daily Telegraph* in 1846, "but not above the knee. Holding a player, carrying the ball is permitted but with one arm only. Running in is permitted but passing with the hands is banned. And if no decision is reached after five afternoons of play, a match will be declared drawn."

**A RUGBY PLAYER "RUNS
WITH THE BALL" IN 1880,
AS IN THE MYTHICAL
STORY ABOUT WILLIAM
WEBB ELLIS**

Two major splits defined the sport we see today. The first came in 1863 when rugby football broke away from the Football Association to form its own game. The Rugby Association wanted to pick up the ball and run with it while they insisted on keeping their affinity with "hacking". Both of these principles were against the essence of football and so the first split was set.

Test match rugby makes its debut

The first rugby union international was staged in 1871 between Scotland and England, in Edinburgh, and won by the Scots in front of around 4,000 spectators – a few thousand less than the Calcutta Cup match would attract today! The teams for this first international were 20-a-side, the test match lasting two periods of 50 minutes, 20 minutes longer than in the modern game. In 1871 another momentous day occurred when the first senior club – Neath RFC – was formed in Wales, and a year later British residents at Le Havre established the first French team.

The formation of the International Rugby Board, where the rules of the game would be enshrined, then followed. The game was very much the preserve of the home nations (England, Scotland, Ireland and Wales) and then in 1895 came rugby's greatest split, when rugby divided into league and union. The greybeards met in Huddersfield and 20 clubs from

**LESLIE WARD IS BEST
KNOWN FOR HIS
CARICATURES OF THE RICH
AND FAMOUS FOUND IN
THE PAGES OF *VANITY FAIR*
MAGAZINE AND SIGNED
WITH HIS ALIAS 'SPY.'
(RIGHT) THIS IS HIS TAKE
ON RUGBY PLAYERS IN THE
GUISE OF LIEUTENANT G H
D'OYLY LYON, RN, IN c.1890**

Cheshire, Lancashire and Yorkshire decided to go their own way and form a new game called rugby league.

The crucial division came about because of money. In rugby league players would be paid to play the new game and the teams would only consist of 13-a-side. Players in working-class areas found it tough to continue playing an amateur game. Unlike some of their richer counterparts in the south, they found it more difficult to play just for the love of the game and what would happen if injury struck? Many of the clubs in the south were made up of ex-public school boys, so the players were in a better position – financially –

HARROW SCHOOL WAS ONE OF THE ENGLISH PUBLIC SCHOOLS SO IMPORTANT IN THE DEVELOPMENT OF THE GAME OF RUGBY UNION

to enshrine the principles of an amateur sport.

France's early love of rugby led to the sport being involved in the Olympics, where the father of the Games, Pierre de Coubertin, made sure it was part of the family. France won the first gold, at the Paris Games in 1900, and although it was again played in 1908 and 1920 it was cut from the list of sports in 1924 with the USA winning the last gold medal, in Paris.

While the divisions were occurring in England – around the turn of the 20th century – the game of rugby union was spreading to countries across the world, most notably to New Zealand and South Africa, where it received an enthusiastic response. Former Rugby schoolboys can be thanked for helping develop the game in many countries as they travelled in the decades after its establishment.

A Home International Championship was first started in 1883, with England as the inaugural winners, in the same year that Ned Haig, the Melrose butcher, devised the truncated version of rugby – sevens. To win that first Championship England claimed victories over Wales, Scotland and Ireland, the Scottish win being England's first triumph north of the border. In 1910 the four became five, when France was admitted to the Championship, welcomed with a 49–14 hammering by Wales. France had to wait until their second Championship – in 1911 – to record their first win. However, it was a controversial kick-off for the French: in 1914 Scotland refused to travel to Paris after allegations that the Scottish players and the English referee were mobbed and assaulted at the end of the previous game in the French capital. Almost 90 years later, in 2000, Italy turned the Five Nations into Six; after the 2006 Championship England still led the way with 25 outright wins.

On the road to the Rugby World Cup

With football starting its own World Cup in 1930, it was inevitable that one day rugby would have their own world championship. As the decades went on the series between New Zealand and South Africa decided the title of unofficial world champion, and between them they totally dominated the rugby world. Scotland and Ireland still have not recorded a single win over New Zealand, while Wales have to go back as far as 1953 to remember their last victory against the All Blacks. It was not until 2003 that England managed to beat both New Zealand and Australia on their own soil in a 12-month period. England's 15–13 victory in Wellington was their first in New Zealand since 1973.

Either side of World War II no-one came close to threatening the domination of New Zealand and South Africa, and even into the 1960s the two sides rarely suffered defeats outside of games against each other. Australia, a country dominated by rugby league, is an infant in rugby union terms, not making a big impact on the world stage until the 1984 tourists completed a Grand Slam while on a European tour, beating England, Wales, Scotland and Ireland.

The New Zealanders, in contrast, toured Europe in 1905 under captain Dave Gallaher. They were first christened The Originals and when they arrived again – in 1924 – the moniker had changed to The Invincibles. The Originals set high standards for teams arriving in Europe from New Zealand, scoring an average of 28 points a game and keeping the opposition scoreless in 23 of their 35 games. The boys at Rugby School may have given birth to the game but The Invincibles defined so many parts of the game we see today. Captained by Cliff Porter, and including the peerless full-back George Nepia, this New Zealand side stayed in Europe for six months winning all 32 of their games – which included four test matches – scoring 838 points and only conceding 116. Nepia played in every game.

The term All Blacks – to describe the New Zealand team – was first used during the 1905 tour when the All Blacks lost 3–0 to Wales, but the true origins of the name are still not known. This was the first side to leave New Zealand for Europe and a report in the *Daily Mail* referred to them as "All Blacks", coining one of the most famous nicknames in the

THE 1905 ORIGINALS TOURING TEAM FROM NEW ZEALAND SHAPED RUGBY UNION IN THE EARLY 20TH CENTURY AND SET NEW STANDARDS FOR THE SIDES IN EUROPE. (BELOW) THEIR FIXTURE LIST SHOWS HOW ARDUOUS THEIR TRIP TO EUROPE WAS

rugby world. In 1905 the first sightings of a haka were also made. The first rugby match on the New Zealand islands took place between Nelson College and Nelson football club in 1870. "Credit for the introduction of rugby to New Zealand goes to Charles John Monro, son of Sir David Monro, Speaker in the House of Representatives from 1860 to 1870," according to the New Zealand Rugby Football Union. "Charles Monro, who was born at Waimea East, was sent to Christ's College, Finchley in England to complete his education and while there he learned the rugby game. On his return to Nelson he suggested that the

FIXTURES.

Date.	Opponent.	Ground.	Result.
Sept. 16	Devon	Exeter	55pt. to 4
,, 20	Cornwall	Redruth	41 ,, 0
,, 23	Bristol	Bristol	41 ,, 0
,, 28	Northampton	Northampton	32 ,, 0
,, 30	Leicester	Leicester	28 ,, 0
Oct. 4	Middlesex	London	34 ,, 0
,, 7	Durham		16 ,, 3
,, 11	The Hartlepools	Hartlepool	63 ,, 0
,, 14	Northumberland	North Shields	31 ,, 0
,, 19	Gloucester City	Gloucester	44 ,, 0
,, 21	Somerset	Taunton	23 ,, 0
,, 25	Devonport Albion	Devonport	21 ,, 3
,, 28	Midland Counties	Leicester	21 ,, 5
Nov. 1	Surrey	Richmond	11 ,, 0
,, 4	Blackheath	Blackheath	,,
,, 7	Oxford Univers'y	Oxford	,,
,, 9	Cambridge ,,	Cambridge	,,
,, 11	Richmond	Richmond	,,
,, 15	Bedford	Bedford	,,
,, 18	Scotland	Edinburgh	,,
,, 22	West of Scotland	Glasgow	,,
,, 25	Ireland	Dublin	,,
,, 29	Munster	Limerick	,,
Dec. 2	England	Crystal Palace	,,
,, 6	Cheltenham	Cheltenham	,,
,, 9	Cheshire	Birkenhead	,,
,, 13	Yorkshire		,,
,, 16	Wales	Cardiff	,,
,, 23	Newport	Newport	,,
,, 26	Cardiff	Cardiff	,,
,, 30	Swansea	Swansea	,,

Total Points up to date 461 15

AGES, WEIGHTS, & HEIGHTS.

BACKS.

	Age. st. lbs ft. in.
W. Wallace	27 ..12 0..5 8
E. Harper	27 ..12 7..5 11
E. Booth	22 ..11 7..5 7½
G. W. Smith	26 ..11 10..5 7
H. Abbott	33 ..13 0..5 10½
F. Roberts	23 ..13 0..6 0
R. Deans	23 ..12 4..5 7
J. Hunter	21 ..13 4..5 6
S. Mynott	26 ..11 8..5 6
W. Stead	29 ..11 0..5 5
G. Gillett	28 ..13 0..6 0

FORWARDS.

	Age. st. lbs ft. in.
D. Gallaher (Capt.)	29 ..13 0..6 0
W. S. Glenn	22 ..12 5..5 10
S. Casey	22 ..12 4..5 10
A. McDonald	22 ..13 0..5 10
W. Johnstone	23 ..13 6..6 0
C. Seeling	22 ..13 7..6 0
G. Nicholson	26 ..13 0..5 10
G. A. Tyler	26 ..13 0..5 11
J. Corbett	22 ..13 0..6 0
F. Glasgow	28 ..15 0..6 5
F. O'Sullivan	25 ..13 3..5 10
J. O'Sullivan	24 ..16 0..5 10
W. Mackrell	22 ..13 3..5 10
W. Cunningham	29 ..14 6..5 11

Manager—MR. DIXON.

local football club try out the rugby rules. The game must have appealed to the club members for they decided to adopt it."

Following the split from rugby league in 1896, rugby waited almost 100 years for its next big step, into the world of professional sport. Staunchly amateur for those 100 years to such an extent that players were banned for life just for being paid to write a book or for daring to even have a trial with a rugby league side, the game went professional overnight. In August 1995 the International Rugby Board declared rugby union "open" after a meeting of the major test playing unions. What became clear at that meeting was that long before the game became professional in 1995, the majority of countries were already paying their players, without sanction.

NEW ZEALAND – HERE IN ACTION AGAINST WALES – HOSTED AND WON THE FIRST RUGBY WORLD CUP, IN 1987, BEATING FRANCE IN THE FINAL

It was vital that the IRB acted in 1995 because if they had done nothing the world's leading players would have almost certainly been signed to an alternative tournament, funded by big business. "The changes are a reflection of the way the game has changed since the seventies when players were not only unpaid but banned from making money even indirectly from the game – for example writing their memoirs or for newspapers," it was reported in *The Daily Telegraph*. "By the early eighties under the counter payments such as 'boot money' from kit manufacturers and inflated expenses became increasingly common."

The Lions make their presence known

Throughout rugby's history the only way the nations of England, Scotland, Ireland and Wales could consistently challenge the giants of New Zealand or South Africa was through the formation of the world famous British and Irish Lions, who did much to promote the game in all corners of the earth. The Lions – a touring side made up of the best players from England, Scotland, Ireland and Wales – first toured in 1888 and have enjoyed a rich history ever since. Early tours were largely Anglo-Welsh affairs, but in 1910 players from all four nations headed to South Africa – under Dr Tom Smythe – losing the test series 2–1.

SOUTH AFRICA CAPTAIN FRANÇOIS PIENAAR PARADES THE WEBB ELLIS CUP AFTER THE SPRINGBOKS WON THE TROPHY IN 1995. THE TOURNAMENT WAS STAGED IN SOUTH AFRICA, TRANSFIXING AND BONDING A NATION THROUGH SPORT

Many feared that professionalism would see an end to the Lions, but they have gone from strength to strength since the mid-1990s. The venerable *Times* writer John Hopkins summed up brilliantly what a Lions' tour is when he said: "A major rugby tour by the British Isles to New Zealand is a cross between a medieval

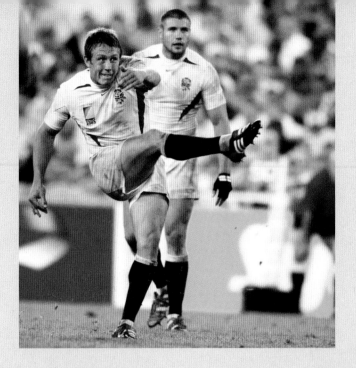

crusade and a prep school outing." The Lions triumphed in their first professional tour in 1997 – under the captaincy of Martin Johnson they won the series 2–1. That victory was not repeated in 2001 when they made the trip to Australia, and when they left New Zealand in 2005 they had suffered the greatest hammering in their history. But those three tours ensured the Lions were here to stay. "The Lions is different in the professional age; it is almost a romantic team rather than a built-up team," said Sir Clive Woodward, who coached the Lions in 2005. He went on, "The Lions are very special. I still think the Lions is a great concept. The supporters over there were just fantastic, they have all had a great trip and hopefully they will do so again in South Africa in four years' time." In 2005 the Lions were followed by 20,000 fans from the UK and Ireland.

JONNY WILKINSON DELIVERED THE WORLD CUP TO ENGLAND FOR THE FIRST TIME IN 2003, KICKING A LAST-MINUTE DROP GOAL AS THEY WON 20–17 AGAINST AUSTRALIA

Calls for a Rugby World Cup first surfaced in the 1970s but were rebuffed as the major nations feared that with a World Cup would come professionalism. Of course they were right. But in the end those members of the old guard who protected amateurism – and opposed a World Cup – were washed over like King Canute, and it is significant that the game went professional just after the 1995 World Cup was held in South Africa. Australia and New Zealand were the key movers in the establishment of a World Cup, and were therefore the obvious choices as joint hosts when it first kicked off in 1987.

Each subsequent World Cup has been bigger than the one before with the 2003 tournament – won by England – breaking a number of records. Just under 2 million spectators watched the 48 games in 2003, with a worldwide television audience of 3.5 billion from 205 countries. The web site www.rugbyworldcup.com had 495 million hits during the tournament, including 44.5 million hits on the day of the Final. The Final itself attracted the largest ever World Cup crowd – 82, 957. "Australia has put on the best ever World Cup, Australia has again done itself proud on the world stage," said Australian Rugby Union Chief Executive John O'Neill, "The atmosphere was extraordinary. Being at the match venues you had to do a double take. At times you read the newspapers and you wondered if there was anything else going on in the world. When people talk about reliving the Olympic spirit (Sydney Olympics) they will talk about reliving the Olympic spirit and the Rugby World Cup spirit." That spirit has remained since 2003 and shows no indication of waning.

THE HISTORY OF POINTS SCORING

Rugby union's points system has evolved since the first one was established in 1890. The changes were:

DATE	TRY	PENALTY
1890–91	1 Point	2 Points
1891–92	2 Points	3 Points
1893–94	3 Points	3 Points
1971–72	4 Points	3 Points
1992–93	5 Points	3 Points

let battle com

ONE

commence

POOL A

POOL B

POOL C

POOL D

Can England double it up?

When Martin Johnson (left) lifted the Webb Ellis Cup in 2003, England became the first side from the northern hemisphere to become world champions. Win it again in 2007 and they would make history as the first side to retain rugby's greatest prize.

In 2007 the holders have been drawn in a group almost exactly the same as the one they overcame four years ago, with the seminal match against South Africa. This time though the game will take place in the 80,000-seater Stade de France, rather than in Perth.

One thing that is for certain is that the England that turns up in 2007 will be radically different from the one that held the World Cup aloft at Sydney's Telstra Stadium on 22 November 2003.

Gone are coach Sir Clive Woodward, captain Martin Johnson and a host of other players including Jason Leonard, Trevor Woodman, Neil Back, Matt Dawson and Will Greenwood.

Without these guiding lights and because of a series of long-term injuries to their hero in 2003 – Jonny Wilkinson – England have endured a rough ride as world champions, and will not go into the 2007 tournament as one of the favourites.

Fourth in the Six Nations Championship in 2004, 2005 and 2006 is unacceptable for an England team that was also humiliated by a seven-match losing run in 2006, a year when they only beat Italy, Wales and South Africa.

ENGLAND AND JOSH LEWSEY (ABOVE) WERE SHACKLED BY SCOTLAND IN 2006 (ABOVE) WHILE TRIES HAVE BECOME A PRECIOUS COMMODITY SINCE 2003 – MARK CUETO GOING OVER FOR ONE AGAINST ITALY (RIGHT)

England 0 Wales 0

But the real indication of how far England had fallen came in November 2006 when Argentina claimed their first-ever victory at Twickenham, and England were left seventh in the world rankings, the lowest position in their history.

This run culminated in Andy Robinson – the coach who replaced Woodward – leaving his post 10 months before the start of the World Cup.

"We've got from first to sixth in the world in 18 months and those rankings do reflect your standing," said former England Captain Fran Cotton, who supports central contracts to help the future of English rugby.

"I think the best idea is for England to select the 100 players they want in the squad, to sign them on and to pay them. The clubs will sign the players that they want to play and we'll go about it that way. There's plenty of other Jonny Wilkinsons coming behind."

ENGLAND KICKED OFF 2006 IN FINE STYLE (LEFT) BEATING WALES 47–13, AND EVEN FOLLOWED THAT UP WITH A 31–16 VICTORY OVER ITALY (ABOVE) BUT AFTER THAT THEY SUCCUMBED TO SEVEN SUCCESSIVE DEFEATS

Springboks hope for a new start

When the draw for the World Cup was made in 2004 South Africa could hardly believe their bad luck, drawn in the same group as the holders England – and the dangerous Samoans. But by 2006 that draw was looking kind to Jake White's South Africa, when they completed a miserable year for England by winning 25–14 at Twickenham. The victory – at the home of English rugby – ended a shocking run of seven successive defeats for South Africa at Twickenham. "Today was a massive win, a huge step forward," said South Africa coach Jake White. "Winning at Twickenham for the first time since 1997 is a huge psychological boost. The big thing of course is the World Cup. Beating the world champions at home 10 months before the World Cup is huge."

White took the calculated gamble of leaving 10 of his best players at home – to rest – before making the trip to Europe to take on not only England but Ireland as well.

SOUTH AFRICA WERE THE ONLY SIDE TO INFLICT DEFEAT ON THE RAMPANT NEW ZEALAND ALL BLACKS IN 2006, SKIPPERED BY JOHN SMIT (RIGHT, BELOW)

MARIUS JOUBERT, ONE OF A GROUP OF EXCITING
YOUNG SPRINGBOKS BACKS WHO HAVE THE ABILITY
TO LIGHT UP THE 2007 WORLD CUP

However it was a gamble that paid off handsomely, not only with the victory at Twickenham but with the discovery of a new generation of Springboks, who are set to light up the 2007 World Cup. Players like François Steyn, Kabamba Floors and Chiliboy Ralepelle were virtual unknowns outside South Africa before the 2006 tour but showed their brilliance, ensuring that White will have a tough selection dilemma in 2007. Ralepelle was handed a further honour at the end of the tour, captaining the side against a World XV, the first black player to skipper South Africa in a major international match.

SOUTH AFRICA'S COACH JAKE WHITE (ABOVE) SURVIVED CALLS FOR HIS RESIGNATION IN 2006...HIS SIDE HAS ONE OF THE WORLD'S BEST LINEOUT EXPONENTS IN VICTOR MATFIELD (RIGHT, IN GREEN)

POOL A – SOUTH AFRICA

POOL A – SOUTH AFRICA

USA Eagles face a mountain to climb

The USA Eagles became the 13th side to qualify for the World Cup, winning an Americas play-off against Uruguay in October 2006. They secured a 75–20 aggregate victory over the Uruguayans to move into pool one. Having been defeated in record fashion by arch rivals Canada in the Americas Two decider, USA entered their two-match play-off series with a lot to prove. "I was very pleased with the end result," USA Rugby's Interim Head Coach Peter Thorburn said. "Our goal was to qualify for the Rugby World Cup, and we are delighted to have achieved that goal. We can now focus on preparing for the tournament next year and the exciting challenge of facing reigning champions England in our opening match." The USA have only won two games, despite making four of the five World Cup finals, both against Japan, in 1987 and 2003.

USA (ABOVE) CELEBRATE THEIR WIN OVER JAPAN IN 2003 WHILE DAVE HODGES (LEFT) WINS SOME LINEOUT BALL AGAINST FRANCE

Beware the rugby warriors of Samoa

Back in 1991 Western Samoa – as they were called then – caused the first and perhaps the biggest upset in Rugby World Cup history, beating Wales 16–13 in Cardiff. This time around – in 2007 – they are faced with a similar task, after being drawn, for the second successive tournament, with holders England, and former winners South Africa.

Michael Jones' Samoans ran through their qualification with ease, beating Fiji and Tonga to take their place in their fifth successive Rugby World Cup finals. Asserting their supremacy in the Pacific Islands, they scored 50 points against Tonga and 36 against Fiji.

STEPHEN SO'OIALO (RIGHT) BRINGS THE EXPERIENCE OF THE GUINNESS PREMIERSHIP TO THE SAMOA SIDE

Off to France, in style

Tonga scored an impressive 13 tries to qualify for the World Cup and take their place alongside England, South Africa, Samoa and USA in Pool A, with a win over Korea. Hudson Tonga'uiha, Fangatapu Apikotoa and wingers Vaea Poteki and Sione Fonua all scored twice as the South Sea Islanders confirmed their spot in France.

TONGA COMPLETE POOL A, AFTER THEIR 83–3 QUALIFICATION VICTORY OVER KOREA, IN AUCKLAND

Fit for a king

The 80,000 capacity Stade de France is the centrepiece of the 2007 Rugby World Cup and will house the crucial Pool A game between England and South Africa on 14 September. Opened in 1998 for the Football World Cup, it earned a special place in the heart of the French nation as it staged the subsequent final and France's 3–0 win over Brazil.

THE COLOUR AND PAGEANTRY OF THE STADE DE FRANCE – ONE OF THE WORLD'S GREATEST STADIUMS – WILL ENSURE AN UNFORGETTABLE RUGBY WORLD CUP

Australia are flying

When Australia lifted the Webb Ellis Cup for a second time in 1999, they won a tournament based in the northern hemisphere. The same was the case eight years earlier when they were victorious for the first time. An omen perhaps for the 2007 campaign as the Wallabies are facing the same conditions this time around.

Back in 1999, the Wallabies were one of the World Cup favourites, but a shocking 2005, when they lost seven consecutive Tests will ensure that they are not one of the fancied teams this time round. That destruction of their reputation was due, in part, to the way their forward pack had been dismantled by some of the other top nations. No one has ever had anything but the highest respect for

their backline, which is set to arrive in Wales as one of the most highly regarded in the world.

And of course the Wallabies have the Gregan

factor. George Gregan will come into the 2007 World Cup as the most-capped player in the history of the game, having passed Jason Leonard's previous high mark in the summer of 2006.

Gregan was rested for the November 2006 tour of Europe so he could be in peak condition when it is time for the trophies to be handed out in France.

John Connolly – appointed Australia coach in 2006 – has set his sights on developing his pack but a 29–29 draw

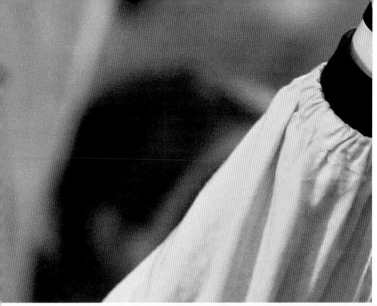

THE WALLABIES WILL BE
CHEERED ON BY LEGIONS OF
FANS IN FRANCE (LEFT) WHILE
THEY WILL BE LOOKING FOR
TRIES LIKE THIS FROM MARK
CHISHOLM (BELOW) AGAINST
ITALY IN 2005

with Wales and a comprehensive defeat to Ireland, a year from the finals will have done a great deal of damage to his ambitions.

At least the Wallabies ended their November 2006 European tour with a victory, beating Scotland 44–15. This was a huge improvement on 2005, when they lost seven consecutive games, an awful run that cost former Australia coach Eddie Jones his job.

"You're not going to go from losing a lot on the trot to winning every game overnight," said Connolly, who

POOL B – AUSTRALIA

confirmed that unlike the New Zealand All Blacks, his Wallaby players would not be afforded a rest during the 2007 Super 14 campaign.

"We're happy with the forwards' progress but with the backs we've got a few steps to go."

MATT GITEAU, SEEN HERE FROM TWO ANGLES, HAS THE ABILITY TO BE ONE OF THE STARS OF THE 2007 WORLD CUP AND COULD TAKE OVER FROM GEORGE GREGAN AS THE AUSTRALIA SCRUM-HALF

Time for Wales to impress

Wales have a World Cup record that bears no resemblance to their place in rugby's history and they have underachieved in almost every one of the five finals.

One of the fabled sides of rugby, their halcyon days of the 1970s – when they ruled the world – came long before the advent of a Rugby World Cup.

After finishing a creditable third in 1987, they proceeded to lose to Samoa in both 1991 and 1999, while suffering at the hands of the New Zealand All Blacks in South Africa in 1995.

But this time round they have been handed a golden chance to make it through beyond the quarter-finals after organisers announced some games would be staged in Wales.

Wales have the distinct advantage of playing their key pool match – against Australia – at their very own Millennium Stadium, where the Wallabies haven't won since 2001.

The last game between the sides in Cardiff – in 2006 –

WALES WILL NEED FLYERS LIKE SHANE WILLIAMS (BELOW) ON TOP FORM IF THEY ARE TO TOPPLE THE WALLABIES AS THEY DID IN 2005 (RIGHT)

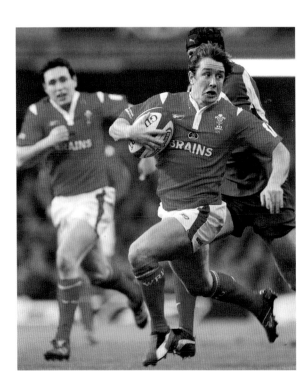

was a stunning 29–29 draw, sealed by a late penalty from fly-half James Hook.

The added edge to the game sees former Wales coach, Scott Johnson, as now the attack specialist for Australia.

"The one that really counts is the World Cup," said Wales captain Gareth Thomas. "We are improving and so are they so hopefully it will be a classic."

Wales finished off 2006 with a 45–10 defeat to New Zealand in Cardiff.

"New Zealand are, at the present time, probably better than anyone else in every department," admitted Wales coach Gareth Jenkins.

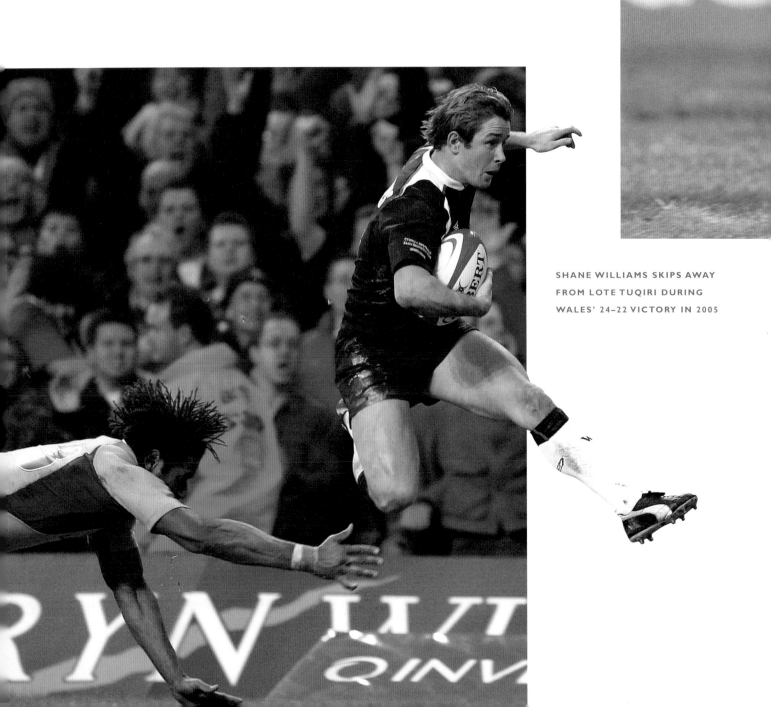

SHANE WILLIAMS SKIPS AWAY
FROM LOTE TUQIRI DURING
WALES' 24–22 VICTORY IN 2005

GAVIN HENSON (ABOVE) IS SET TO BE ONE OF THE HIGH PROFILE PLAYERS AT THE WORLD CUP WHILE GARETH THOMAS (LEFT) WILL BE PLAYING IN HIS FOURTH, AND ALMOST CERTAINLY LAST, FINALS

Ready to fulfill their destiny

Fiji are masters of the Sevens game but have yet to make the breakthrough in the 15-a-side code that their skills richly deserve.

Quarter-finalists in 1995, they will be dangerous outsiders in 2007, especially if their pack can get much-needed balls for their devastating backline.

This time round they will need to target the games against Wales and Australia, and they have been helped with the draw as they are playing Wales in Nantes, rather than Cardiff.

One thing that is for sure is that they have one of the most explosive players at the tournament with wing Rupeni Caucaunibuca, who is playing in his second World Cup.

Caucau, as he is better known, came so close to sending Fiji into the last eight in 2003, scoring two tries in the crucial game against Scotland, only to see the Scots snatch a 22–20 victory in the closing minutes.

"He could be a superstar," said Fiji's coach at the 2003 World Cup Mac McCallion. "He's got a great future – he's probably got more potential than any other player that I've been involved with or seen."

API NAEVO (TOP), ALFRED ULUINAYAU (ABOVE) AND VILIMONI DELASAU (RIGHT) DID MUCH TO KEEP THE FIJIAN FANS HAPPY IN 2003, JUST FAILING – BY TWO POINTS – TO MAKE THE QUARTER-FINALS OF THE WORLD CUP

Fiji

POOL B

Canucks hope to turn the tables

When Canada lost to Wales in 2006 at the Millennium Stadium, Canada coach Ric Suggitt claimed it would be totally different the next time the sides meet, in the World Cup.

At least Canada will not have to travel to Cardiff for their pool game, which is in Nantes, and will have a crop of players – unavailable in 2006 – for the World Cup.

"We will beat Wales, that's what we are going to the World Cup for," said Suggitt, after seeing his side lose 61–26 to Wales in Cardiff.

"It's a realistic aim and that's what we are building towards."

"This was a good experience for our guys, I asked them to be bold and throw caution to the wind, and when that happens mistakes can be made."

The Canucks stormed through their qualification rounds, almost embarrassing their near rivals, USA, with a massive 56–7 victory.

BOTH DEAN VAN CAMP AND BRODIE HENDERSON SCORED TRIES FOR CANADA IN 2003

Try machine heading for France

Japan may be targeting just one win in the 2007 World Cup but one thing is for sure: they will have a world record holder in their side, in the shape of Daisuke Ohata.

The wing scored his 69th test try when Japan romped through their qualification pool beating Hong Kong 52–3 and Korea 54–0 at the end of 2006.

Their improvement since 2003 is evident in those results, but a place in the quarter-finals still looks beyond them, even though they have recently appointed All Blacks legend John Kirwan as their coach.

"I am very pleased for the boys and Japan," said Kirwan. "There was lot of pressure on us before the game but we can now think about the World Cup. The players did their nation proud."

The Japanese will be strong contenders to host the 2015 World Cup, after just missing out – to New Zealand – for the 2011 event.

IN DAISUKE OHATA (TOP LEFT) JAPAN HAVE THE WORLD'S LEADING TRY SCORER, WHILE IN 2003 THEY HAD TAKASHI TSUJI (LEFT) AS SCRUM-HALF

POOL B Stadium

Venue of legends

The 37,000-capacity Le Stade in Toulouse is one of the stadiums being used in Pool B and should be a sea of colour for the clash between France and Namibia. It will also play host to Japan v Fiji and New Zealand v Romania. The football stadium was formerly a venue for bullfighting and was used in the 1998 Football World Cup.

Motoring to The World Cup

The New Zealand All Blacks will arrive at the 2007 World Cup as the hottest favourites in the history of the tournament, and it will be a major shock if they do not win. Over a two-year period they have broken records and stunned the opposition wherever they go. Only South Africa have beaten New Zealand in those 23 games and coach Graham Henry sees the Springboks as a big threat in 2007.

"South Africa will be a real challenge in the World Cup," said Henry. "They have got a lot of guys at home who didn't come on their European tour in 2006. I think Jake White (South Africa coach) got it right. They had a lot of young guys come through on the trip."

"And they are not intimidated by the All Blacks. They think they can handle us."

Henry has assembled not only a world-class playing squad but has brought in Steve Hansen (from Wales)

ANTON OLIVER (LEFT) IN NEW ZEALAND'S UNSUCCESSFUL 2003 CAMPAIGN, BUT FOUR YEARS LATER HE WILL BE HOPING TO GO ONE STAGE BETTER

and Wayne Smith (from Northampton) as his coaches. And in 2005 and 2006 Henry set about developing a squad of 30 players who could conquer the world. Henry was criticised for a rotation policy that saw a number of changes, although as his side kept winning he was able to keep going.

CHRIS MASOE (BELOW) AND CASEY LAULALA (ABOVE) ARE TWO ALL BLACKS WHO HAVE EMERGED IN THE LAST TWO YEARS AS THE ALL BLACKS BECAME THE WORLD'S NUMBER ONE SIDE

LUKE McALISTER LEADS THE ALL BLACKS THROUGH IRELAND'S DEFENCE AS THEY STARTED THEIR 2006 SEASON WITH A VICTORY. THEY NEVER LOOKED BACK, LOSING JUST ONE MATCH IN THE YEAR, AND THAT AFTER THEY HAD BEEN CROWNED TRI-NATIONS CHAMPIONS

SCRUM-HALF BYRON KELLEHER (LEFT) AND SECOND ROW ALI WILLIAMS (RIGHT) WILL BE KEEN MEMBERS OF NEW ZEALAND'S WORLD CUP SIDE, AND THEY'LL BE HOPING TO KEEP THEIR LEGIONS OF SUPPORTERS IN GOOD VOICE

Scots head for France with hope in their hearts

France only clinched the 2006 RBS Six Nations crown on the final day of the championship, but there was no doubt over the title for the tournament's most-improved team – Scotland.

The Scots had endured one of the most miserable periods in their history either side of the 2003 World Cup, but along came new coach Frank Hadden in 2005 to turn round their fortunes and make them contenders for a place in the semi-finals this time around.

Scotland managed just one victory – over Italy – in two Six Nations tournaments under Australian Matt Williams, before Hadden took over. If we presume Scotland won't complete their first-ever win over New Zealand at the World Cup, even if the game is in Edinburgh, the key game for the Scots is likely to come in St-Étienne, on 29 September, when they take on Italy.

SEAN LAMONT (RIGHT) IS ONE OF THE MOST POTENT WEAPONS AT THE DISPOSAL OF SCOTLAND COACH FRANK HADDEN

The fact that Frank Hadden's Scotland will already have played New Zealand could have a huge bearing on his selection. Many would favour a weakened side going out at Murrayfield to face New Zealand, saving the big guns for the Italy game that could guarantee them a quarter-final berth. Scotland did worry their fans a little with their final game of 2006, a 40–15 defeat at home to an Australian side that had already lost to Ireland and drawn with Wales. "It is an extremely young side, and that gives me tremendous confidence with the next World Cup looming in 2007," said Hadden. "Scotland's history has seen one or two occasions of tremendous over-achievement, and I am hoping this is the start of one for us."

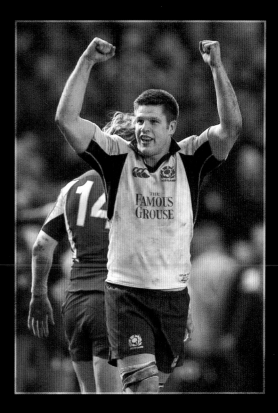

Azzurri aim to rattle the big boys

Italy started their build-up to the 2007 Rugby World Cup with an impressive set of performances a year before that will make them dangerous outsiders in France. The Italians will also be buoyed by an excellent recent record against World Cup opponents Scotland, completing their first Six Nations win in 2000 over them, and repeating the trick four years later. They had been the whipping boys of the Six Nations in between, but their fortunes have taken an upward curve since the appointment of Pierre Berbizier in 2005, taking over from John Kirwan. In November 2006 they lost to Argentina, pushed Australia hard and beat Canada 41–6.

Berbizier felt the 18–18 draw against Wales in the 2006 RBS Six Nations was a big breakthrough for his side. "This gives a mark of respect for the Italian team on the international scene," Berbizier said. "To hold Wales here is a big achievement and we now have the respect of the other teams. We are now showing what we are capable of achieving."

Italy became the seventh side to qualify for the 2007 World Cup, with a convincing 67–7 result against Russia.

MAURO BERGAMASCO (RIGHT) AND CAPTAIN MARCO BORTOLAMI (CENTRE, WITH HEAD GUARD) LEAD AN EVER-GROWING LIST OF WORLD CLASS PLAYERS IN THE ITALIAN SIDE, MAKING THEM A TEAM WHO COULD CAUSE A SHOCK IN 2007

PABLO CANAVOSIO SCORES AND THEN CELEBRATES A TRY AS ITALY CLAIMED THEIR FIRST-EVER AWAY POINT IN THE SIX NATIONS, DRAWING 18–18 WITH WALES IN 2006

POOL C

Life is tough for the minnows

Romania will be dangerous foes for Scotland, having beaten them twice, in 1984 and 1991, and coming into the tournament as European Nations Cup (Second Division of the Six Nations) champions. Romania's chances of staging an upset have been hampered by the decision to stage the match at Murrayfield. How much more even would this game be if it was staged in Marseille or Bordeaux? Instead the minnows are dealt yet another bad hand by the organisers, and left to travel to the home of Scottish rugby, to face Scotland in a World Cup match!

LUCIAN SIRBU AND OVIDIU TONITA OF ROMANIA (ABOVE) CELEBRATE WINNING THE WORLD CUP POOL MATCH AGAINST NAMIBIA IN 2003, WHERE THEY WERE LED BY CAPTAIN ROMEO GONTINEAC (BELOW) AND IN FRANCE THEY WILL FACE PORTUGAL WHO QUALIFIED FOR THE FIRST TIME

The final finalists

Portugal – coached by Tomaz Morais – became the twentieth and last side to qualify for the World Cup with a thrilling, two-leg, 24–23 victory over Uruguay.

DESPITE LOSING THE SECOND LEG IN MONTEVIDEO (BELOW) THE PORTUGUESE PLAYERS CELEBRATE AN HISTORIC VICTORY WITH AN OVERALL AGGREGATE ADVANTAGE OF JUST ONE POINT, ENOUGH TO TAKE THEM TO THE FINALS

POOL C Stadium

Magnificent Murrayfield

Murrayfield, the home of Scottish rugby will be home to two matches in the World Cup, including the crucial Scotland v New Zealand clash on 23 September. The stadium now holds 67,500 fans, after being reopened in 1994 following a redevelopment costing £37million. It still holds the record for the biggest attendance at a rugby game, when a crowd of 104,000 watched Scotland play Wales in 1975.

YANNICK JAUZION
(ABOVE), DESCRIBED BY
SOME AS THE WORLD'S
BEST PLAYER, HAS THE
ABILITY TO MASTERMIND
FRANCE'S FIRST RUGBY
WORLD CUP TITLE

FRANCE'S PLAYMAKER,
FRÉDÉRIC MICHALAK
(RIGHT) WILL BE CRUCIAL
TO FRANCE'S EFFORTS,
MISSING A HUGE PART OF
THE 2006–07 SEASON
AFTER INJURING HIS KNEE
IN NOVEMBER 2006

POOL D – FRANCE

France look to capitalise on their home advantage

The most successful northern hemisphere country in the history of the Rugby World Cup, France, will be straining every sinew to go one better than their appearance in the 1987 final.

Since that epic final 20 years ago, France have only once failed to make at least the semi-final, in 1991, pulling off a series of breathtaking wins in the last four finals.

Their most memorable was the 43–31 victory over New Zealand in 1999 as they fell behind before scoring 33 points to seven from the All Blacks to storm home.

In 2003 England were their semi-final conquerors, beating Les Bleus 24–7, but since that time France have won a Grand Slam and an RBS Six Nations Championship.

In the November 2006 matches France suffered two morale-sapping defeats to New Zealand, yet finished off the series with a win over Argentina.

But coach Bernard Laporte is urging his side to go back to their roots for the World Cup, and show the flair which makes them famous – and feared – throughout the rugby world.

"The intentions are all there, but we need to be more ambitious. We need to let ourselves go more," says Laporte, who knows his side have the honour of playing in the first match of the World Cup, against Argentina.

"The All Blacks are definitely above the rest but, hopefully, the World Cup will be another story than this November tour."

Team Manager Jo Maso added: "We went into the game (against Argentina) with two objectives, to win and to win in style. We won and we played with style for an hour, now we have to work to keep the rhythm for a whole match."

FRANCE'S MAGNIFICENT FANS WILL BE IN GOOD VOICE AND COLOURFULLY DRESSED FOR THE WORLD CUP, AND WILL BE HOPING TO SEE PLAYERS LIKE DAMIEN TRAILLE (LEFT) AND FLORIAN FRITZ CELEBRATING SOME GREAT TRIES

THE TWO YANNICKS, NYANGA (LEFT) AND JAUZION (RIGHT) HAVE THE ABILITY TO BE THE HEARTBEAT OF THE FRANCE TEAM AT THIS WORLD CUP. NYANGA IS ONE OF THE BRIGHTEST PROSPECTS IN EUROPEAN RUGBY, WHILE JAUZION HAS THE CAPABILITY TO MASTERMIND THE FRANCE WORLD CUP CAMPAIGN

Ireland ripe for a cracking World Cup

In Ireland's history there have been many great days. The Grand Slam of 1948, the recent Triple Crowns of 2004 and 2006, but there aren't too many dates competing for the worst day – most people would accept that was on 20 October, 1999. On that day Ireland were forced to travel to Lens for a quarter-final play-off against Argentina on a night of high drama. Ireland lost that game, 28–24, and their place in the world's top-eight countries. Reputations were ruined on that fateful night in northern France and the Irish even had to suffer the embarrassment of being forced to qualify for the 2003 tournament. It means that even to this day, Ireland are one nation that will never underestimate the Argentinians.

Ireland face the Argentinians again in 2007 but this time as one of the form nations in the northern hemisphere, confirmed by a magnificent and unbeaten run in November 2006.

Australia, South Africa and the Pacific Islanders all arrived in Dublin and were all beaten comprehensively.

Those victories left Ireland as the world's third best side, according to the IRB Rankings, leaving coach Eddie O'Sullivan trying his best to play down his side's World Cup hopes.

"It was a good victory against a strong Australia team. They weren't experimenting and put their best foot forward for this game," said O'Sullivan. "I don't take too much notice of where we are in the game. It doesn't change where you are in the overall scheme of things."

"The rankings are a barometer of where a team are. You can only draw conclusions from it over a period of time."

"Ireland have been in and around the top five for the last couple of years. We are third now but if we lost a couple of games we'd slip right back down."

IRELAND HAVE ESTABLISHED THEMSELVES AS ONE OF THE WORLD'S BEST SIDES UNDER THE CAPTAINCY OF BRIAN O'DRISCOLL

SHANE HORGAN IS ONE OF THE MOST
IMPROVED PLAYERS IN A POTENT IRELAND
BACKLINE THAT COULD CAUSE A SHOCK OR
TWO AT THE WORLD CUP. HERE HE LEAVES
DAFYDD JAMES ON THE GROUND AS HE ELUDES
THE WELSH DEFENCE TO SCORE A TRY AT
LANDSDOWNE ROAD IN THE RBS SIX NATIONS

Beware the dangerous Los Pumas

Of all the outsiders in this Rugby World Cup, it is the Argentinians who are most likely to give the so-called 'big boys' a bloody nose. They have a history of upsets from their quarter-final play-off victory over Ireland in 1999 to the victory over world champions England, at Twickenham, in 2006. That win left Argentina ranked as the seventh best side in the world. For a side made up almost exclusively of European-based players, France will seem like a home from home. They will kick off the 2007 World Cup, playing hosts France, as they did in 1999 and 2003. Led by inspirational captain Agustin Pichot, the Pumas hope that another impressive World Cup campaign will lead to them being admitted to either the RBS Six Nations or Tri-Nations Championship, after 2006 wins over England and Italy. "I think that the rugby people must think about Argentina. Our current performance justifies our inclusion in the main international tournaments." said Pichot. Who could deny him?

GONZALO TIESI (ABOVE RIGHT), SCORING AGAINST WALES, IS ONE OF A GROWING NUMBER OF ARGENTINIAN PLAYERS FROM THE GUINNESS PREMIERSHIP, WHILE (RIGHT) FEDERICO MARTIN ARAMBURU CRASHES OVER FOR A TRY AGAINST WORLD CUP OPPONENTS IRELAND. BELOW ARGENTINA TAKE ON NEW ZEALAND IN JUNE 2006, COMING CLOSE TO BEATING THE ALL BLACKS, FINALLY LOSING 25–19

Third time lucky for the Namibians

No one could question Namibia's place at the 2007 World Cup. Despite losing by record margins in 2003 they completed one of the most torturous routes to this year's tournaments, finally emerging as the best side in Africa, behind the Springboks. After clearing a number of qualifying hurdles, they finally clinched their place with a two-leg

victory over Morocco in Windhoek, securing a 52–15 aggregate victory.

"I am delighted that we have achieved our goal of qualifying for the Rugby World Cup 2007," said Namibia captain Kees Lensing. "Knowing that Morocco would throw everything at us we could not afford to defend our advantage. Therefore, I am really pleased that we played some positive rugby and scored four tries in the process."

NAMIBIA CAPTAIN KEES LENSING IS LOOKING FORWARD TO LEADING HIS SIDE INTO THIS YEAR'S WORLD CUP, HOPEFULLY AVOIDING SOME OF THE HAMMERINGS THEY TOOK IN 2003

THE GEORGIA TEAM (TOP) CELEBRATE THEIR WIN OVER PORTUGAL WHILE PLAYERS DAVIT ZIRAKASHVILI (LEFT) AND MAMUKA GORGODZE SHOW HOW ELATED THEY ARE TO QUALIFY FOR THE WORLD CUP

Let's go round again

There were scenes of jubilation in Lisbon when Georgia became the 18th team to qualify for the 2007 World Cup, after winning their two-legged battle with Portugal. The sides drew 11–11 in the Portugese capital, but the Georgians' 14-point lead from that first leg booked their World Cup place.

The Georgians made their World Cup debut in 2003, qualifying into England and South Africa's group in Australia.

They failed to win a game in 2003, but their presence in Australia was a breath of fresh air.

"We need experience. We are a baby," said Zara Kassachvili, the vice-president of the Georgian federation.

The jewel of southern France

The southernmost city to stage matches at the Rugby World Cup, Marseilles will be a sea of rugby on the weekend of October 6 and 7 as the famous football stadium hosts two quarter-finals, deciding the fate of the sides in all four pools.

Earlier in the tournament New Zealand and Italy will do battle in the French port, while France will visit there on 30 September to take on the Georgians.

PART heroes in

FROM BORTOLAMI TO WHITE...THE MEN SET TO MAKE

T W O
waiting

THE HEADLINES AT THE 2007 RUGBY WORLD CUP

Marco Bortolami – Italy

MARCO BORTOLAMI – **Second row** – **Italy** A large part of the rugby world is dying for one of the so-called smaller nations to make the breakthrough into the quarter-finals of the Rugby World Cup. Italy is one of the nations on the verge of that breakthrough, one of the reasons being their charismatic and imposing leader, Marco Bortolami. A lineout expert, Bortolami became Italy's youngest captain when he led his country against Japan in 2004. Bortolami was a crucial absentee when Italy played Wales for a place in the 2003 World Cup quarter-finals, but this time around his experience – after moving to Gloucester in the summer of 2006 – will be crucial to their hopes.

Career Details Test debut against Namibia, June 2001 • Club in England, Gloucester • Born in Padova, 12 June 1980.

Career Details Test debut against England, June 2003 • Province, in New Zealand, The Crusaders • Born in Leeston, 5 March 1982.

CALLING MR WONDERFUL... THE WORLD'S BEST PLAYER IN 2005, DAN CARTER WILL BE CRUCIAL TO NEW ZEALAND'S CHANCES AT THE WORLD CUP

BREAKTHROUGH BOYS... IS THIS THE TOURNAMENT WHEN MARCO BORTOLAMI'S (OPPOSITE) ITALY WILL MAKE THEIR FIRST MOVE INTO THE QUARTER-FINALS?

DAN CARTER – **Outside-half** – **New Zealand**

In every generation come players who can mesmerise, change the course of a game, or even a World Cup. Such a player – in 2007 – is the Canterbury Crusader, Dan Carter. The outside-half first announced himself on the world stage in 2005 when his performances with the boot – and with ball in hand – were a big factor in New Zealand's record-breaking series win over the Lions. An exemplary goalkicker, he made his debut, aged 21, against Wales in 2003, scoring 20 points, and in his first 30 Tests he averaged almost 16 points a game.

HEROES IN WAITING

Rupeni Caucaunibuca – Fiji

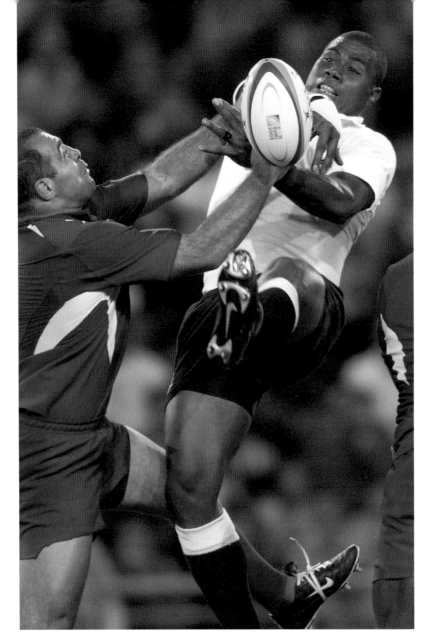

RUPENI CAUCAUNIBUCA – **Wing** – **Fiji** At the last two World Cups the quarter-finalists have been almost exactly the same eight teams. So if one of the so-called minnows is going to make a breakthrough in 2007 it will need some of the ability of Fiji's Rupeni Caucaunibuca to lead the charge. Caucau as he is better known is a mould-breaking runner, tough to stop – with his powerful frame – and with an enviable turn of speed, which sees him complete the 100 metres in less than 11 seconds.

ROCKET MAN…RUPENI CAUCAUNIBUCA, OR CAUCAU TO HIS FRIENDS, MADE A HUGE IMPACT IN 2003. WATCH OUT FOR HIS OWN BRAND OF FIREWORKS IN 2007

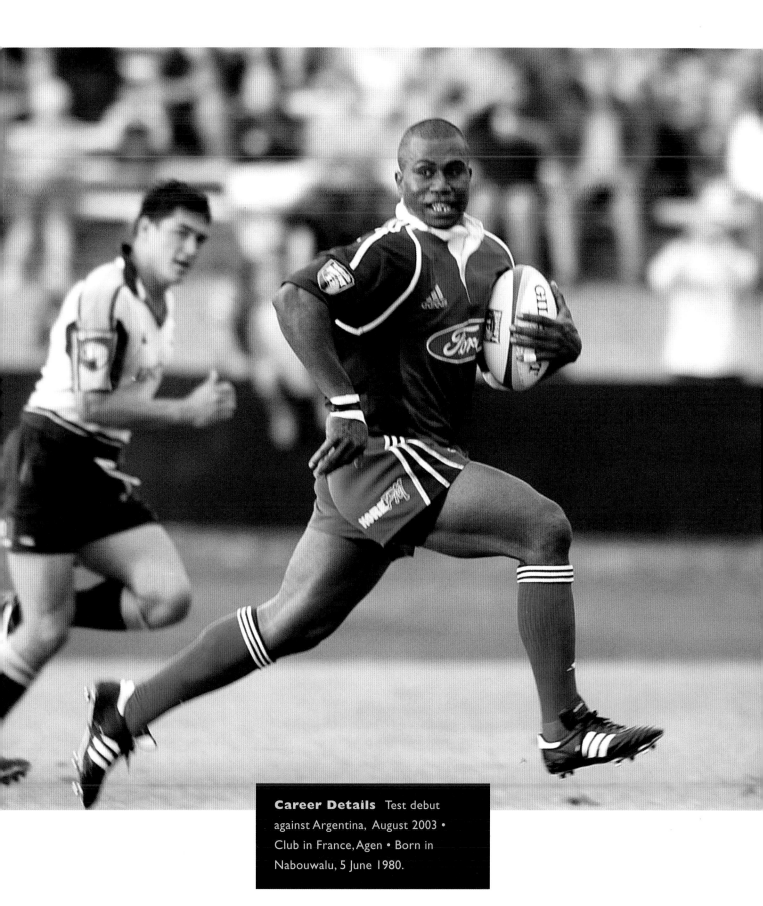

Career Details Test debut against Argentina, August 2003 • Club in France, Agen • Born in Nabouwalu, 5 June 1980.

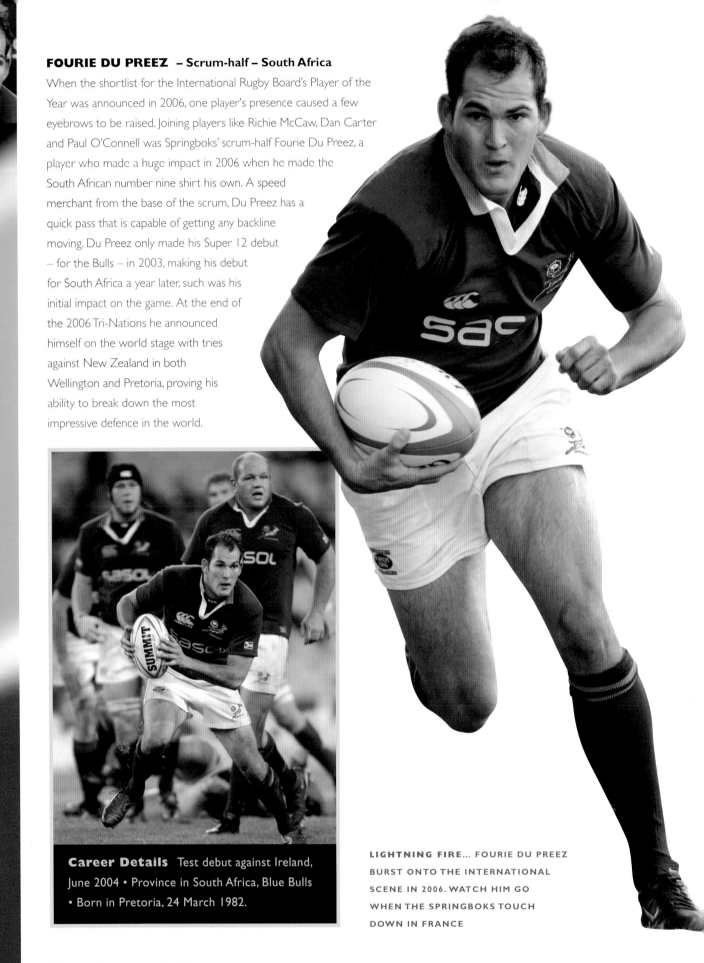

FOURIE DU PREEZ – Scrum-half – **South Africa**

When the shortlist for the International Rugby Board's Player of the Year was announced in 2006, one player's presence caused a few eyebrows to be raised. Joining players like Richie McCaw, Dan Carter and Paul O'Connell was Springboks' scrum-half Fourie Du Preez, a player who made a huge impact in 2006 when he made the South African number nine shirt his own. A speed merchant from the base of the scrum, Du Preez has a quick pass that is capable of getting any backline moving. Du Preez only made his Super 12 debut – for the Bulls – in 2003, making his debut for South Africa a year later, such was his initial impact on the game. At the end of the 2006 Tri-Nations he announced himself on the world stage with tries against New Zealand in both Wellington and Pretoria, proving his ability to break down the most impressive defence in the world.

Career Details Test debut against Ireland, June 2004 • Province in South Africa, Blue Bulls • Born in Pretoria, 24 March 1982.

LIGHTNING FIRE... FOURIE DU PREEZ BURST ONTO THE INTERNATIONAL SCENE IN 2006. WATCH HIM GO WHEN THE SPRINGBOKS TOUCH DOWN IN FRANCE

HEROES IN WAITING

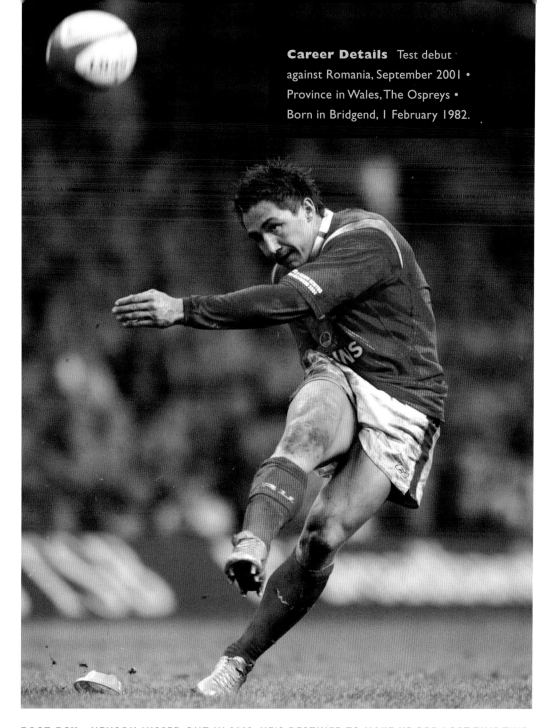

Career Details Test debut against Romania, September 2001 • Province in Wales, The Ospreys • Born in Bridgend, 1 February 1982.

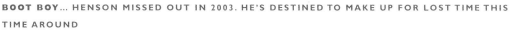

BOOT BOY... HENSON MISSED OUT IN 2003. HE'S DESTINED TO MAKE UP FOR LOST TIME THIS TIME AROUND

GAVIN HENSON – Centre – Wales When Gavin Henson stepped up to land a monster penalty against England in 2005, his place in Welsh folk history was guaranteed. Not only did the nerveless 45-metre kick ensure an 11–9 win but it set Wales on course for their first Grand Slam in 27 years. Another star who can play international rugby outside-half, centre or full-back, Henson was the International Rugby Board's Young Player of the Year in 2001. A solid defender, his deft touch with ball in hand sets him apart. An awful 2005–06 season when Henson was blighted by injury and suspension interrupted his impressive career, which had seen him help the Ospreys to the Celtic League title in 2005, and saw him make his Lions debut in New Zealand.

HEROES IN WAITING

YANNICK JAUZION – **Centre** – **France**   Most rugby players would settle for speed, flair or the ability to make bulldozing runs. Yannick Jauzion, the France centre, manages all three. He emerged onto the world stage as a key part of the Toulouse side that reached the Heineken Cup final in 2003, 2004 and 2005. Jauzion – a destructive passer who can open up any defence – missed the 2006 RBS Six Nations through injury, but was an integral part of the France team that won Grand Slams in 2002 and 2004.

SIMPLY THE BEST...
ACCLAIMED BY
MANY AS THE
WORLD'S BEST
PLAYER, NOW IS
THE TIME FOR
YANNICK JAUZION
TO PROVE IT

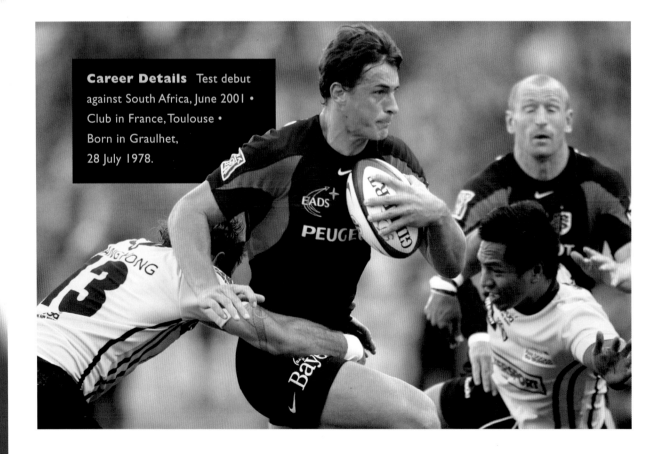

Career Details   Test debut against South Africa, June 2001 • Club in France, Toulouse • Born in Graulhet, 28 July 1978.

CHRIS LATHAM – **Full-back** – **Australia** A full-back with devastating ability, Chris Latham won the ultimate honour in Australian rugby – in 2006 – after being awarded the John Eales Medal. Latham – who made his debut in 1998 – was the first back to receive the award, voted for by the Australian players. When he takes the field in France it will be his third World Cup. A gifted runner, Latham runs the angles that most rugby players can only dream of. The Queensland Red was voted Australian Super 12 Player of the Year three times, in 2000, 2003 and 2004.

FLYING HIGH... WITHOUT PEER IN THE AUSTRALIAN TEAM, THE WORLD CUP IS COMING AT THE PERFECT TIME FOR CHRIS LATHAM

Career Details Test debut against France, November 1998 • Province, in Australia, The Queensland Reds • Born in Narrabri, 8 September 1975.

Chris Latham – Australia

Josh Lewsey – England

JOSH LEWSEY – Full back / Wing – England After England won the World Cup in 2003 their squad suffered a minor disintegration. Players like captain Martin Johnson, Neil Back and Jason Leonard retired, and Jonny Wilkinson sustained a series of long-term injuries as England slipped to seventh in the world rankings. In the ensuing years there were countless changes but one man remained; Josh Lewsey. The London Wasps full back was the only player to be selected in the 22 Tests following the World Cup victory. At home either on the wing or at full back, Lewsey is a former army officer cadet, who struggled to balance life as a professional rugby player with that of a soldier. Lewsey made his debut on the infamous Tour to Hell undertaken by England in 1998, when they were thumped by Australia, New Zealand and South Africa. That trip was the making of players like Lewsey and Jonny Wilkinson. Unflappable under the high ball, Lewsey's pace and powerful running style make him one of the best finishers in the rugby world.

ENGLANDS MR RELIABLE, JOSH LEWSEY... EVADES THE TACKLE OF BRYAN HABANA (RIGHT) AND LEAVES DEFENDERS STANDING (BELOW) DURING A BRACE OF GAMES AGAINST POOL A RIVALS SOUTH AFRICA AT TWICKENHAM AT THE END OF 2006. ENGLAND WON THE FIRST ENCOUNTER AND SOUTH AFRICA THE SECOND

Career Details Test debut against New Zealand, June 1998 • Club in England, London Wasps • Born in Bromley, 30 November 1976

**BRIAN LIMA – Utility-back –
Samoa** Most rugby players see playing in the Rugby World Cup as the culmination of their careers. But in 2007 Brian Lima looks certain to become the first man to play in an incredible five World Cups. Lima was on duty when Samoa turned the rugby world on its head – in 1991 – when they beat Wales in Cardiff and he'll be there again to take on England this time around. Nicknamed The Chiropractor because of his ability to make bone-crunching tackles, Lima is an on-field leader who inspires his side and can turn a game with one of his legendary big hits. Lima was the youngest player at the 1991 tournament and could now be the oldest, 16 years later, never having missed a World Cup match for his beloved Samoa.

HIT PARADE... BRIAN LIMA MAY BE ARRIVING AT THE WORLD CUP AS ONE OF THE OLD MEN BUT HE CAN STILL HIT WITH THE BEST AS DERICK HOUGAARD FOUND OUT IN 2003 (BELOW)

Career Details Test debut against Wales, October 1991 • Club in England, Bristol • Born in Apia, 25 January 1972.

Richie McCaw – New Zealand

Career Details Test debut against Ireland, November 2001 • Province, in New Zealand, The Crusaders • Born in Oamaru, 31 December 1980.

RICHIE McCAW – Openside flanker – New Zealand When the voting closed for the IRB Player of the Year 2006, one thing was certain: Richie McCaw would be the winner. Of course there was a shortlist of five, but no one in the rugby world actually considered that they would vote for anyone else. The New Zealand skipper is the key to the All Blacks' hopes at the World Cup. If he rules the roost at the breakdown, they have the backs to beat any side in the world.

RAMPANT RICHIE... HAS THERE BEEN A BETTER NO 7 IN THE HISTORY OF THE GAME? WE'LL FIND OUT AT THE WORLD CUP

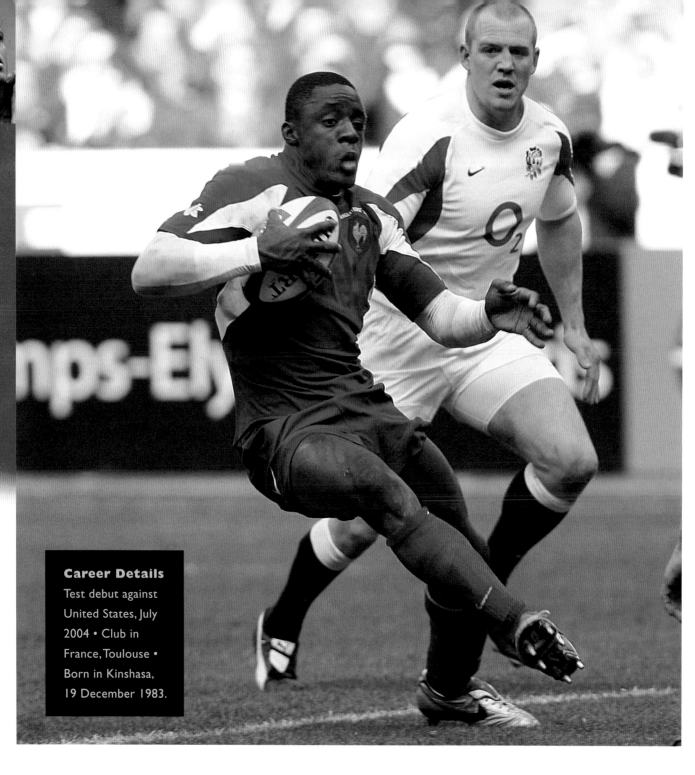

Yannick Nyanga – France

Career Details

Test debut against United States, July 2004 • Club in France, Toulouse • Born in Kinshasa, 19 December 1983.

YANNICK NYANGA – Openside flanker – France France has a long and successful tradition of African-born sportsmen and women starring in their national sides. Think of Serge Betsen in the 2003 World Cup or Marie-José Pérec striding to three Olympic golds in the 1990s. The latest in a long line of Africans to move into the France rugby team is the dynamic Yannick Nyanga, who was born in the Democratic Republic of the Congo, but now plays for Toulouse. He only made his debut in 2004, but his athletic ability and rock-solid defence quickly marked him out as a world star.

STAR IN THE MAKING... YANNICK NYANGA HAS COME FROM OBSCURITY – IN THE LAST FOUR YEARS – TO MAKE THE FRENCH TEAM. BUT AS ENGLAND FOUND OUT IN 2006 (ABOVE) HE HAS THE ABILITY TO LIVE WITH THE BEST

HEROES IN WAITING

PAUL O'CONNELL – Second row –

Ireland Any side looking to make an impact at the 2007 World Cup will need men of strength in the pack and the greatest example could be found in the green of Ireland. Paul O'Connell is a second row forward to rival any on the planet. A man of Munster, O'Connell made his Ireland debut in 2002, establishing himself on the world stage at the World Cup the following year. Guaranteed to win his own ball at lineout time, O'Connell is a big threat on opposition ball, a fearsome scrummager and a real danger in the loose.

Paul O'Connell – Ireland

THE O TEAM... PAUL O'CONNELL IS HITTING FORM JUST IN TIME TO BE A COLOSSUS AT THE 2007 WORLD CUP

Career Details
Test debut against Wales, February 2002 • Province in Ireland, Munster • Born in Limerick, 20 October 1979.

IN BOD WE TRUST... BRIAN
O'DRISCOLL IS ONE OF THE
STARS OF EUROPEAN RUGBY
THE WORLD CUP PRESENTS
HIM WITH THE CHANCE TO
BECOME A WORLD GREAT

Career Details Test
debut against Australia, June
1999 • Province in
Ireland, Leinster •
Born in Dublin,
21 January
1979.

BRIAN O'DRISCOLL – Centre – Ireland Every side
needs their talisman and if Ireland are going to have a
successful 2007 World Cup campaign, captain Brian O'Driscoll
will have to hit some of the best form of his career. A sensational
player for both Leinster and Ireland, O'Driscoll had the unenviable task of
taking over the national captaincy from the legendary Keith Wood – in 2003
– and the Leinster man led them to Triple Crowns in
2004 and 2006. He made his Ireland debut in 1999 and
quickly established himself as a world star, his elusive
running style bringing him a hat trick against France, in
Paris in 2000, as his side won 27–25. He was made Lions
captain in 2005, but survived less than two minutes of
the first test, missing the rest of the tour with a career-
threatening shoulder injury.

HEROES IN WAITING

Career Details Test debut against Korea, November 1996 • Club in Japan, Kobe Steel • Born in Osaka, 11 November, 1975.

DAISUKE OHATA – Wing – Japan

Only two players in the history of rugby union have scored more than 60 tries in Test matches. One is the famous David Campese while the other is Japanese speedster Daisuke Ohata. The Japan wing overtook Campese's world record – which had stood for ten years – in May 2006 when he scored three tries against Georgia. A wing or occasionally a centre, Ohata – who plays for Kobe Steel in the Japanese Top League – captained Japan when they won the Asian qualifying tournament in November 2006, to make it to the 2007 World Cup.

TRY MACHINE... DAISUKE OHATA WILL STRETCH HIS LEAD OVER THE WORLD'S BEST AT THE WORLD CUP

Daisuke Ohata - Japan

95

Career Details Test debut against Japan, May 1995 • Club in France, Toulouse • Born in Ogwr, 27 July 1974.

HEROES IN WAITING

GARETH THOMAS –

Utility back – Wales No Wales rugby player has scored more international tries than the man affectionately called Alfie Thomas the length and breadth of the country. Thomas made his Wales debut against Japan in 1995 and went on to play in three World Cups, captaining his country in 2003, in Australia. Equally at home in the centre, on the wing or at full-back, he has been a crucial part of the Wales set-up. Thomas started his career at his hometown club Bridgend, moving on to Celtic Warriors, Cardiff and Toulouse. He lost the Wales captaincy in 2006, after battling back from a health scare that threatened his career when he suffered a ruptured artery in his neck.

WELSH WARRIOR... THOMAS EPITOMISES THE SPIRIT OF THE WELSH NATION WHETHER IN THE WHITE OF TOULOUSE (LEFT) OR WITH THE DRAGON ABOVE HIS HEAD (ABOVE)

Jason White – Scotland

Career Details Test debut against England, April 2000 • Club in England, Sale Sharks • Born in Edinburgh, 17 April 1978.

JASON WHITE – Blindside flanker – **Scotland** It is no coincidence that the letters that make up the word HIT figure prominently in the name Jason White. The unassuming Scotland captain was the key reason for the country's re-emergence in 2006, when they beat both world champions England and Six Nations Championship winners France. One of the best blindside flankers in the world, he is famous for his steamroller tackles, and renowned as one of the hardest hitters in the rugby world. A big threat at the back of the lineout, he played a crucial part in Sale winning the first English championship in their history, in 2006. The Scotland Player of the Year in 2005–06, his turnovers have the capability of turning matches.

FLOWER OF SCOTLAND... JASON WHITE HAS
HELPED RESTORE THE PRIDE BACK TO THE
SCOTLAND TEAM AND THEY TURN OUT TO BE ONE
OF THE DARK HORSES FOR THE WORLD CUP

P A R T
the path to

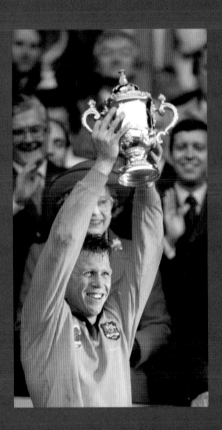

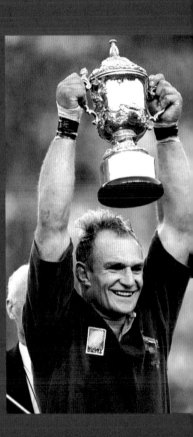

**1987
NEW
ZEALAND**

**1991
AUSTRALIA**

**1995
SOUTH
AFRICA**

THREE
glory
COMPLETE WITH ALL THE ESSENTIAL STATISTICS

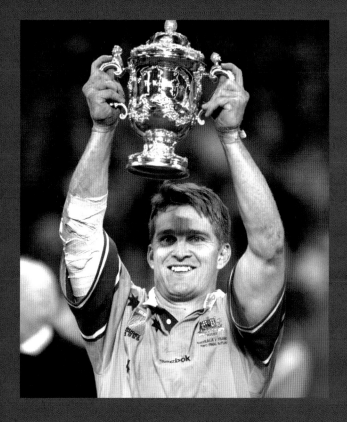

**1999
AUSTRALIA**

**2003
ENGLAND**

The All Blacks first to conquer

The Rugby world was a very different place in 1987, but some things don't change as the New Zealand All Blacks were confirmed as the best team in the world, lifting the Webb Ellis Cup for the first time.

In a tournament staged in New Zealand and Australia the All Blacks stormed through the competition scoring an impressive 298 points in their six games and never seriously being troubled once. France got closest to beating David Kirk's team, but even they succumbed by 20 points in the final.

Grant Fox stood like a colossus over this first World Cup, scoring 126 points – a record that still stands today.

"Lifting the cup was how people must feel at the top of Everest. They only have 20 minutes there and won't ever be back," said Kirk. "The only way back is down. But that melancholy was overwhelmed by joy."

Wales were the leading Home Nation, finishing third, a position they failed to beat in the following four tournaments. The 16 sides who competed were invited, rather than having to qualify as they to do today.

ROBERT JONES OF WALES CLEARS HIS LINES AS THE WELSH OVERCOME AUSTRALIA FOR THIRD PLACE (ABOVE)

ENGLAND STARTED THE FIRST WORLD CUP BADLY, LOSING 19–6 TO AUSTRALIA (RIGHT). A DISAPPOINTING TOURNAMENT FOR ENGLAND ENDED WHEN THEY WERE BEATEN IN THE QUARTER-FINALS BY WALES

THE NEW ZEALAND TEAM
PERFORM THE HAKA
PRIOR TO THEIR SEMI-
FINAL CLASH WITH
WALES (ABOVE)

NEW ZEALAND CAPTAIN
DAVID KIRK CRASHES
OVER IN THE FINAL (LEFT)
AND LATER LIFTS THE
TROPHY FOLLOWING THE
ALL BLACKS' 29–9
VICTORY OVER FRANCE
(RIGHT)

NEW ZEALAND 1987

1987 Stat Attack

The Pool Stages

POOL A

AUSTRALIA	19–6	ENGLAND
JAPAN	18–21	USA
ENGLAND	60–7	JAPAN
AUSTRALIA	47–12	USA
ENGLAND	34–6	USA
AUSTRALIA	42–23	JAPAN

POOL B

CANADA	37–4	TONGA
IRELAND	6–13	WALES
WALES	29–16	TONGA
IRELAND	46–19	CANADA
WALES	40–9	CANADA
IRELAND	32–9	TONGA

POOL C

NEW ZEALAND	70–6	ITALY
FIJI	28–9	ARGENTINA
NEW ZEALAND	74–13	FIJI
ARGENTINA	25–16	ITALY
FIJI	15–18	ITALY
N ZEALAND	46–15	ARGENTINA

POOL D

ROMANIA	21–20	ZIMBABWE
FRANCE	20–20	SCOTLAND
FRANCE	55–12	ROMANIA
SCOTLAND	60–21	ZIMBABWE
FRANCE	70–12	ZIMBABWE
SCOTLAND	55–28	ROMANIA

THE KNOCKOUT STAGES
QUARTER-FINALS

NEW ZEALAND	30–3	SCOTLAND
FRANCE	31–16	FIJI
AUSTRALIA	33–15	IRELAND
WALES	16–3	ENGLAND

SEMI-FINALS

AUSTRALIA	24–30	FRANCE
NEW ZEALAND	49–6	WALES

THIRD-PLACE MATCH

AUSTRALIA	21–22	WALES

THE 1987 WORLD CUP FINAL

NEW ZEALAND	29–9	FRANCE

NEW ZEALAND

J GALLAGHER, J KIRWAN, W TAYLOR,
J STANLEY, C GREEN, G FOX, D KIRK
(CAPT), S MCDOWELL, S FITZPATRICK,
J DRAKE, G WHETTON, M PIERCE,
A WHETTON, M JONES, W SHELFORD

SCORERS

TRIES JONES, KIRK, KIRWAN **CONS** FOX
PENS FOX 4 **DROP GOALS** FOX

FRANCE

S BLANCO, D CAMBERABERO, P SELLA,
D CHARVET, P LAGISQUET, F MESNEL,
P BERBIZIER, P ONDARTS, D DUBROCA
(CAPT), JP GARUET, J CONDOM,
A LORIEUX, D ERBANI, E CHAMP,
L RODRIGUEZ

SCORERS

TRIES BERBIZIER **CONS** CAMBERABERO
PENS CAMBERABERO

1987 WORLD CUP RECORDS

MOST POINTS
126 G FOX (NZ), 82 M LYNAGH (AUS)
62 G HASTINGS (SCOT)

MOST TRIES
6 C GREEN (NZ), 6 J KIRWAN (NZ)

MOST DROP GOALS
3 J DAVIES (WALES)

MOST POINTS IN A MATCH
30 D CAMBERABERO (FRANCE V
ZIMBABWE), 27 G HASTINGS (SCOTLAND V
ROMANIA), 26 G FOX (NZ V FIJI)

AUSTRALIA, WITH DAVID CAMPESE (TOP) IN GREAT FORM, ENJOYED A BREATHTAKING QUARTER-FINAL AGAINST IRELAND, BEFORE GOING ON TO LIFT THE CUP. AGAINST IRELAND THEY FELL BEHIND TO A LATE GORDON HAMILTON TRY BUT IN INJURY TIME MICHAEL LYNAGH (ABOVE) STOLE THE SHOW WITH A SENSATIONAL SCORE, WHILE SCOTLAND AND DAVID SOLE (RIGHT) LOST 9–6 TO ENGLAND IN THE SEMI-FINAL

Wallabies climb to rugby's summit

After two countries hosted the first World Cup it was decided to bring the second tournament to the northern hemisphere and share it amongst the five nations of Wales, England, Scotland, Ireland and France. England hosted the first game – which they lost to New Zealand – and due to the pool system were also around at the end, managing to achieve the unique distinction of also losing the last – the final – to Australia.

In between, Will Carling's England endured one of the most tortuous routes to any World Cup final, having to beat France – in Paris – and Scotland – in Edinburgh – to make it.

But in that final – when the 1991 competition's one millionth spectator came through the turnstiles – they were kidded by David Campese and his fellow Wallabies to abandon their narrow game plan, that relied on their juggernaut pack, to play a more expansive style …and right into the hands of Australia.

In the final Australia, captained by Nick Farr-Jones (above), got home courtesy of one try, from Tony Daly.

New Zealand failed in their attempt to win back-to-back titles, losing to Australia in the semi-finals.

Ireland's Ralph Keyes ended as the tournament's leading scorer with 68 points.

AUSTRALIA CAPTAIN NICK FARR-JONES DECLARED IT "A DREAM COME TRUE" WHEN HE LIFTED THE WEBB ELLIS CUP (LEFT) JUST BEFORE HE AND HIS TEAM-MATES DIVED INTO THE BATHS AT TWICKENHAM (BELOW) BRINGING THE TROPHY WITH THEM! "EVERYTHING YOU'VE EVER DONE IN RUGBY BECOMES WORTHWHILE WHEN YOU WIN THE WORLD CUP – AND WHAT WE SHOWED WAS ALL ABOUT COURAGE," FARR-JONES ADDED AFTER THE 12–6 VICTORY OVER ENGLAND IN THE FINAL

1991 Stat Attack

The Pool Stages

POOL A

NEW ZEALAND	18–12	ENGLAND
ITALY	30–9	USA
NEW ZEALAND	46–6	USA
ENGLAND	36–6	ITALY
ENGLAND	37–9	USA
NEW ZEALAND	31–21	ITALY

POOL B

SCOTLAND	47–9	JAPAN
IRELAND	55–11	ZIMBABWE
IRELAND	32–16	JAPAN
SCOTLAND	51–12	ZIMBABWE
SCOTLAND	24–15	IRELAND
JAPAN	52–8	ZIMBABWE

POOL C

AUSTRALIA	32–19	ARGENTINA
WESTERN SAMOA	16–13	WALES
AUSTRALIA	9–3	WESTERN SAMOA
WALES	16–7	ARGENTINA
AUSTRALIA	38–3	WALES
WESTERN SAMOA	35–12	ARGENTINA

POOL D

FRANCE	30–3	ROMANIA
CANADA	13–3	FIJI
FRANCE	33–9	FIJI
CANADA	19–11	ROMANIA
ROMANIA	17–15	FIJI
FRANCE	19–13	CANADA

THE KNOCKOUT STAGES
QUARTER-FINALS

FRANCE	10–19	ENGLAND
SCOTLAND	28–6	WESTERN SAMOA
IRELAND	18–19	AUSTRALIA
NEW ZEALAND	29–13	CANADA

SEMI-FINALS

SCOTLAND	6–9	ENGLAND
NEW ZEALAND	6–16	AUSTRALIA

THIRD-PLACE MATCH

NEW ZEALAND	13–6	SCOTLAND

THE 1991 WORLD CUP FINAL

ENGLAND	6–12	AUSTRALIA

ENGLAND
J WEBB, S HALLIDAY, W CARLING (CAPT), J GUSCOTT, R UNDERWOOD, R ANDREW, R HILL, J LEONARD, B MOORE, J PROBYN, P .ACKFORD, W DOOLEY, M SKINNER, M TEAGUE, P WINTERBOTTOM

SCORERS
PENS WEBB 2

AUSTRALIA
M ROEBUCK, D CAMPESE, J LITTLE, I HORAN, R EGERTON, M LYNAGH, N FARR-JONES (CAPT), T DALY, P KEARNS, E MCKENZIE, R MCCALL, J EALES, S POIDEVIN, T COKER, V OFAHENGAUE

SCORERS
TRIES DALY   **CONS** LYNAGH
PENS LYNAGH 2

1991 WORLD CUP RECORDS

MOST POINTS
68 R KEYES (IRELAND), **66** M LYNAGH (AUSTRALIA), **61** G HASTINGS (SCOTLAND)

MOST TRIES
4 B ROBINSON (IRELAND V ZIMBABWE), **3** T WRIGHT (NZ V USA), I TUKALO (SCOTLAND V ZIMBABWE) AND J-B LAFOND (FRANCE V FIJI)

MOST POINTS IN A MATCH
24 J WEBB (ENGLAND V ITALY), **23** R KEYES (IRELAND V ZIMBABWE)

Rainbow nation rises to the occasion

SOUTH AFRICA'S DREAM OF A PLACE IN THE 1995 WORLD CUP FINAL ALMOST ENDED IN RAIN-LASHED KING'S PARK, DURBAN (BOTTOM) WHEN THEY SCRAPED PAST FRANCE 19–15. THE GAME WAS DELAYED 90 MINUTES UNTIL THE DELUGE STOPPED AND WORKERS WERE EVEN FORCED ON TO THE FIELD (BELOW) TO MOP UP THE WATER

South Africa spent more than a decade in the sporting wilderness, banned from competition because of the apartheid regime. So after the boycott was lifted and they returned to international rugby – in 1992 – there was only one place to hold the Rugby World Cup, in the Rainbow Nation.

And they didn't disappoint, with a classic World Cup that captivated not only the continent of Africa but also the whole of the rugby world.

The Springboks were destined to win their own World Cup and after the first final to go into extra time, they triumphed in a pulsating clash with New Zealand.

The All Blacks had blown England away in the semi-finals with an incredible display that announced Jonah Lomu to the world of rugby.

Holders Australia disappeared in the quarter-finals when France once again made the last four. France succumbed to a rampant South African side that seemed to have fate on their side as well as an expectant nation.

THIS WAS THE MOMENT WHEN JOEL
STRANSKY SENT A NATION INTO
RAPTURES (LEFT) WITH THIS INJURY-TIME
DROP GOAL FOR SOUTH AFRICA, AGAINST
NEW ZEALAND, WINNING THE 1995 WORLD
CUP. THE WEBB ELLIS CUP WAS PRESENTED
(RIGHT) BY THE COUNTRY'S PRESIDENT
NELSON MANDELA TO THE TEAM'S
CAPTAIN FRANÇOIS PIENAAR

SOUTH AFRICA 1995

1995 Stat Attack

The Pool Stages

POOL A

SOUTH AFRICA	27–18	AUSTRALIA
CANADA	34–3	ROMANIA
SOUTH AFRICA	21–8	ROMANIA
AUSTRALIA	27–11	CANADA
AUSTRALIA	42–3	ROMANIA
SOUTH AFRICA	20–0	CANADA

POOL B

WESTERN SAMOA	42–18	ITALY
ENGLAND	24–18	ARGENTINA
WESTERN SAMOA	32–26	ARGENTINA
ENGLAND	27–20	ITALY
ITALY	31–25	ARGENTINA
ENGLAND	44–22	WESTERN SAMOA

POOL C

WALES	57–10	JAPAN
NEW ZEALAND	43–19	IRELAND
IRELAND	50–28	JAPAN
NEW ZEALAND	34–9	WALES
NEW ZEALAND	145–17	JAPAN
IRELAND	24–23	WALES

POOL D

SCOTLAND	89–0	IVORY COAST
FRANCE	38–10	TONGA
FRANCE	54–18	IVORY COAST
SCOTLAND	41–5	TONGA
TONGA	29–11	IVORY COAST
FRANCE	22–19	SCOTLAND

THE KNOCKOUT STAGES
QUARTER-FINALS

FRANCE	36–12	IRELAND
SOUTH AFRICA	42–14	WESTERN SAMOA
ENGLAND	25–22	AUSTRALIA
NEW ZEALAND	48–30	SCOTLAND

SEMI-FINALS

SOUTH AFRICA	19–15	FRANCE
NEW ZEALAND	45–29	ENGLAND

THIRD-PLACE MATCH

ENGLAND	9–19	FRANCE

THE 1991 WORLD CUP FINAL

SOUTH AFRICA	15–12	NEW ZEALAND
(AFTER EXTRA TIME)		

SOUTH AFRICA

A JOUBERT, J SMALL (B VENTER 97), J MULDER,
H LE ROUX, C WILLIAMS, J STRANSKY, J VAN
DER WESTHUIZEN, O DU RANDT,
P ROSSOUW, B SWART (G PAGEL 68), K WIESE,
H STRYDOM, F PIENAAR (CAPT), M ANDREWS
(R STRAEULI 90), R KRUGER

SCORERS
PENS STRANSKY 3
DROP GOALS STRANSKY 2

NEW ZEALAND

G OSBORNE, J WILSON(M ELLIS 55), F BUNCE,
W LITTLE, J LOMU, A MEHRTENS, G BACHOP,
C DOWD (R LOE 83), S FITZPATRICK (CAPT),
O BROWN, I JONES, R BROOKE, M BREWER
(J JOSEPH 40), Z BROOKE, J KRONFELD

SCORERS
PENS MEHRTENS 3
DROP GOALS MEHRTENS

1995 WORLD CUP RECORDS

MOST POINTS
112 T LACROIX (FRANCE),
104 G HASTINGS (SCOTLAND),
84 A MEHRTENS (NEW ZEALAND)

MOST TRIES
7 M ELLIS (NEW ZEALAND),
J LOMU (NEW ZEALAND)

MOST POINTS IN A MATCH
45 S CULHANE (NEW ZEALAND V JAPAN),
44 G HASTINGS (SCOTLAND V IVORY COAST)

Wallabies hit double top

Australia made rugby history in 1999. Not only did they win the World Cup, but became the first side to lift the Webb Ellis Cup twice, following their triumph at Twickenham in 1991.

This time the celebrations started 200 miles down the M4 in Cardiff as the Millennium Stadium hosted the fourth World Cup final.

Defence was king in 1999 as the Wallabies won rugby's greatest prize in a tournament where they only conceded one try, and that was against the USA in the pool stages, when many of their frontline players were rested.

New Zealand had been everyone's favourites, playing sublime rugby until they met a rampant French side in the semi-final. The All Blacks powered to a 24–10 lead before France staged one of the greatest comebacks in the history of the World Cup to claim the victory.

The French were unable to produce anything like that form in the final as Australia shut down their running game for a comprehensive victory.

GEORGE GREGAN (RIGHT) IS ECSTATIC AFTER AUSTRALIA CLAIMED THEIR SECOND WORLD CUP, WHILE THE WALLABIES AND FRANCE STAND TOE-TO-TOE IN THE FINAL (BELOW)

After a magnificent display through the competition Tim Horan (below) was confirmed as the Player of the Tournament in 1999. "Horan had a wonderful month and not even Jonah Lomu could touch him for contribution to his side's performance," said former Wallabies captain Nick Farr-Jones in Sydney's *Daily Telegraph*. "He invariably found openings in midfield, got over the advantage line and looked to me like he wanted to get his hands on the ball a lot. Two years ago, I admit I thought Tim Horan was washed up and the best years of his rugby career were behind him. Today, he wears the worthy mantle of World Cup player of the tournament."

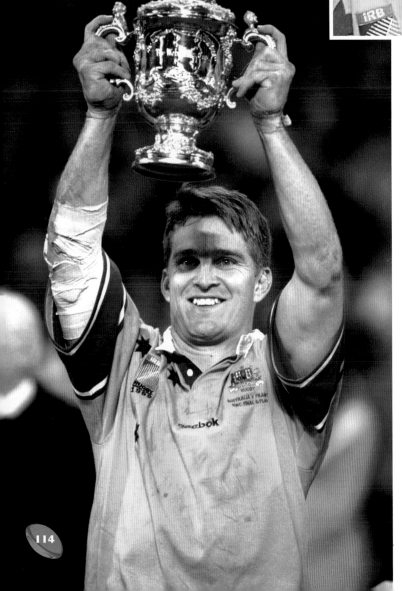

AUSTRALIA WING JOE ROFF GETS THE PARTY STARTED IN THE DRESSING ROOM AFTER THE WALLABIES CLINCHED THEIR SECOND WORLD CUP, FOLLOWING A 35–12 VICTORY OVER FRANCE. THE WIN WAS EARNED AT THE MILLENNIUM STADIUM (RIGHT), OPENED FOR THE 1999 TOURNAMENT

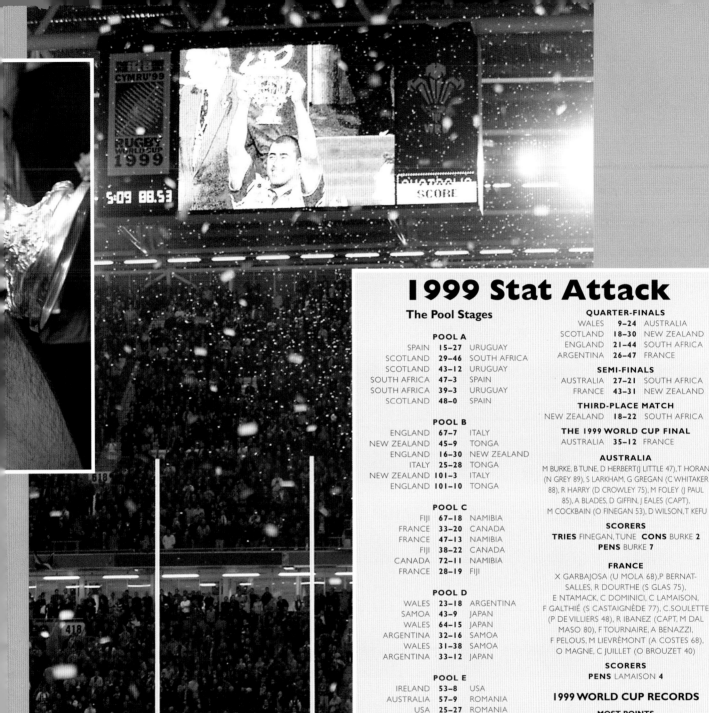

1999 Stat Attack

The Pool Stages

POOL A

SPAIN	15–27	URUGUAY
SCOTLAND	29–46	SOUTH AFRICA
SCOTLAND	43–12	URUGUAY
SOUTH AFRICA	47–3	SPAIN
SOUTH AFRICA	39–3	URUGUAY
SCOTLAND	48–0	SPAIN

POOL B

ENGLAND	67–7	ITALY
NEW ZEALAND	45–9	TONGA
ENGLAND	16–30	NEW ZEALAND
ITALY	25–28	TONGA
NEW ZEALAND	101–3	ITALY
ENGLAND	101–10	TONGA

POOL C

FIJI	67–18	NAMIBIA
FRANCE	33–20	CANADA
FRANCE	47–13	NAMIBIA
FIJI	38–22	CANADA
CANADA	72–11	NAMIBIA
FRANCE	28–19	FIJI

POOL D

WALES	23–18	ARGENTINA
SAMOA	43–9	JAPAN
WALES	64–15	JAPAN
ARGENTINA	32–16	SAMOA
WALES	31–38	SAMOA
ARGENTINA	33–12	JAPAN

POOL E

IRELAND	53–8	USA
AUSTRALIA	57–9	ROMANIA
USA	25–27	ROMANIA
IRELAND	3–23	AUSTRALIA
AUSTRALIA	55–19	USA
IRELAND	44–14	ROMANIA

THE KNOCKOUT STAGES
QUARTER-FINAL PLAY OFFS

SCOTLAND	35–20	SAMOA
ENGLAND	45–24	FIJI
ARGENTINA	28–24	IRELAND

QUARTER-FINALS

WALES	9–24	AUSTRALIA
SCOTLAND	18–30	NEW ZEALAND
ENGLAND	21–44	SOUTH AFRICA
ARGENTINA	26–47	FRANCE

SEMI-FINALS

AUSTRALIA	27–21	SOUTH AFRICA
FRANCE	43–31	NEW ZEALAND

THIRD-PLACE MATCH

NEW ZEALAND	18–22	SOUTH AFRICA

THE 1999 WORLD CUP FINAL

AUSTRALIA	35–12	FRANCE

AUSTRALIA

M BURKE, B TUNE, D HERBERT (J LITTLE 47), T HORAN (N GREY 89), S LARKHAM, G GREGAN (C WHITAKER 88), R HARRY (D CROWLEY 75), M FOLEY (J PAUL 85), A BLADES, D GIFFIN, J EALES (CAPT), M COCKBAIN (O FINEGAN 53), D WILSON, T KEFU

SCORERS
TRIES FINEGAN, TUNE **CONS** BURKE 2
PENS BURKE 7

FRANCE

X GARBAJOSA (U MOLA 68), P BERNAT-SALLES, R DOURTHE (S GLAS 75), E NTAMACK, C DOMINICI, C LAMAISON, F GALTHIÉ (S CASTAIGNÈDE 77), C.SOULETTE (P DE VILLIERS 48), R IBANEZ (CAPT, M DAL MASO 80), F TOURNAIRE, A BENAZZI, F PELOUS, M LIEVRÈMONT (A COSTES 68), O MAGNE, C JUILLET (O BROUZET 40)

SCORERS
PENS LAMAISON 4

1999 WORLD CUP RECORDS

MOST POINTS
102 G QUESADA (ARGENTINA), 101 M BURKE (AUSTRALIA), 97 J DE BEER (SOUTH AFRICA)

MOST TRIES
8 J LOMU (NEW ZEALAND), 6 J WILSON (NEW ZEALAND)

MOST POINTS IN A MATCH
36 T BROWN (NEW ZEALAND V ITALY), 36 P GRAYSON (ENGLAND V TONGA)

Cup heads back to the north

It took until the fifth tournament, but finally a team from the northern hemisphere lifted the Webb Ellis Cup – Clive Woodward's England, led by the indomitable Martin Johnson.

Coming into the tournament as the world's number one team after picking up a Grand Slam earlier in the year, England built up an irresistible momentum that took them through to the World Cup Final.

The final itself – against Australia – was breathtaking.

After the lead changed hands, it was finally settled with just over a minute of extra time to go by a drop goal from Jonny Wilkinson, which sailed through the posts off his weaker right foot.

"It was a huge effort by the entire squad of players, coaches and backroom staff, everybody. Thanks to the fans, they were incredible," said Johnson.

"I can't say enough about the team, because we had the

lead and we lost it but we came back. And I can't say enough about Wilko at the end."

"I'm just so happy for the players, they've put their heart and soul into it. It couldn't have been any closer and I'm just happy I'm on the right side."

Elton Flatley's heroics were almost forgotten in the pandemonium that followed Wilkinson's late kick. After a Lote Tuqiri try took Australia ahead, and England fought back, it was Flatley's boot that tied it up in the second half, to send the game into extra time.

New Zealand once again failed to cope with the pressure of a World Cup. Storming through the pool stages with a mammoth 282 points from four games they faltered in the semi-finals, losing to Australia 22–10. The defeat cost All Blacks coach John Mitchell his job as an unforgiving public turned on the man at the top.

IMANOL HARINORDOQUY FLOATS THROUGH THE AIR FOR A TRY (OPPOSITE BELOW) TO SEND FRANCE THROUGH TO THE WORLD CUP SEMI-FINAL, WHILE (OPPOSITE ABOVE) PHIL VICKERY TURNED HERO WITH A TRY WHEN IT LOOKED AS THOUGH ENGLAND WOULD LOSE TO SAMOA. (ABOVE) WALES AND ENGLAND BATTLE IT OUT FOR A PLACE IN THE LAST FOUR

Wales showed the green shoots of recovery, pushing both England and New Zealand hard before succumbing in a pulsating quarter-final to England, 28–17.

The rugby world was delighted to see a World Cup debut for the Georgians, but less pleased to see the hammerings dealt to Namibia, Tonga and Romania, which again demonstrated that the gulf between the game's top ten and the rest was growing.

ELTON FLATLEY'S WORLD-CLASS KICKING PERFORMANCE KEPT AUSTRALIA IN THE WORLD CUP FINAL, WITH 12 OF THEIR 17 POINTS. HE WAS ICE COOL WITH THE BOOT AS AUSTRALIA CLAWED THEIR WAY BACK IN THE SECOND HALF (ABOVE). JASON ROBINSON SCORES ENGLAND'S ONLY TRY SENDING THEM INTO A 14–5 LEAD (ABOVE RIGHT)

2003 Stat Attack

The Pool Stages

POOL A

AUSTRALIA	24–8	ARGENTINA
IRELAND	45–17	ROMANIA
ARGENTINA	67–14	NAMIBIA
AUSTRALIA	90–8	ROMANIA
IRELAND	64–7	NAMIBIA
ARGENTINA	50–3	ROMANIA
AUSTRALIA	142–0	NAMIBIA
ARGENTINA	15–16	IRELAND
NAMIBIA	7–37	ROMANIA
AUSTRALIA	17–16	IRELAND

POOL B

FRANCE	61–18	FIJI
SCOTLAND	32–11	JAPAN
FIJI	19–18	USA
FRANCE	51–29	JAPAN
SCOTLAND	39–15	USA
FIJI	41–13	JAPAN
FRANCE	51–9	SCOTLAND
JAPAN	26–39	USA
FRANCE	41–14	USA
SCOTLAND	22–20	FIJI

POOL C

SOUTH AFRICA	72–6	URUGUAY
ENGLAND	84–6	GEORGIA
SAMOA	60–13	URUGUAY
SOUTH AFRICA	6–25	ENGLAND
GEORGIA	9–46	SAMOA
SOUTH AFRICA	46–19	GEORGIA
ENGLAND	35–22	SAMOA
GEORGIA	12–24	URUGUAY
SOUTH AFRICA	60–10	SAMOA
ENGLAND	111–13	URUGUAY

POOL D

NEW ZEALAND	70–7	ITALY
WALES	41–10	CANADA
ITALY	36–12	TONGA
NEW ZEALAND	68–6	CANADA
WALES	27–20	TONGA
ITALY	19–14	CANADA
NEW ZEALAND	91–7	TONGA
ITALY	15–27	WALES
CANADA	24–7	TONGA
NEW ZEALAND	53–37	WALES

THE KNOCKOUT STAGES
QUARTER-FINALS

NEW ZEALAND	29–9	SOUTH AFRICA
AUSTRALIA	33–16	SCOTLAND
FRANCE	43–21	IRELAND
ENGLAND	28–17	WALES

SEMI-FINALS

| NEW ZEALAND | 10–22 | AUSTRALIA |
| FRANCE | 7–24 | ENGLAND |

THIRD-PLACE MATCH

| NEW ZEALAND | 40–13 | FRANCE |

THE 2003 WORLD CUP FINAL

AUSTRALIA **17–20** ENGLAND*
* AFTER EXTRA TIME

AUSTRALIA

M ROGERS (J ROFF), W SAILOR, S MORTLOCK, E FLATLEY, L TUQIRI, S LARKHAM (M GITEAU), G GREGAN (CAPT), B YOUNG (M DUNNING), B CANNON (J PAUL), A BAXTER, J HARRISON, N SHARPE (D GIFFIN), G SMITH, P WAUGH, D LYONS (M COCKBAIN)

SCORERS
TRIES TUQIRI **PENS** FLATLEY **4**

ENGLAND

J ROBINSON, J LEWSEY (I BALSHAW), W GREENWOOD, M TINDALL (M CATT), B COHEN, J WILKINSON, M DAWSON, T WOODMAN, S THOMPSON, P VICKERY (J LEONARD), M JOHNSON (CAPTAIN), B KAY, R HILL (L MOODY), N BACK, L DALLAGLIO

SCORERS
TRIES ROBINSON **PENS** WILKINSON **4**
DROP GOALS WILKINSON

2003 WORLD CUP RECORDS

MOST POINTS
113 J WILKINSON (ENG), **103** F MICHALAK (FR), **100** E FLATLEY (AUS)

MOST TRIES
7 D HOWLETT (NZ), M MULIAINA (NZ), **6** J ROKOCOKO (NZ), **5** W GREENWOOD (ENG), C LATHAM (AUS), J LEWSEY (ENG) M ROGERS (AUS), L TUQIRI (AUS)

BBQ THAT!

JONNY WILKINSON KICKED
THE DROP GOAL THAT
BROUGHT THE WORLD CUP
TO ENGLAND, COMPLETING
A 20–17 VICTORY. AT THE
FINAL WHISTLE BEN
COHEN HUGS WILKINSON
AND LAWRENCE DALLAGLIO
JOINS THE CELEBRATION
(RIGHT) WHILST IN THE
STAND AN ENGLISH FAN
HAS A MESSAGE FOR THE
LOSING SIDE (ABOVE)

PART FOUR

inside the game

1 LONGEST NAME: Joost van der Westhuizen, South Africa (below)

2 FIRST TO PLAY IN FOUR WORLD CUPS: Gareth Rees, Canada 1987–1999

3 MOST CONS: Gavin Hastings, Scotland 39 (below)

4 MOST POINTS IN RWC HISTORY: Gavin Hastings, Scotland 227 (above)

5 HEAVIEST: Joeli Veitayaki, Fiji – 136Kg

6 MOST TRIES: Jonah Lomu, New Zealand, 15 (below)

7 SHORTEST: Earl Va'a, Samoa – 166cm (right)

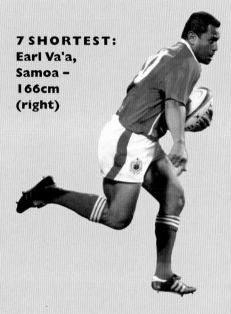

8 THE LIGHTEST: Desmond Snyders, Namibia 68Kg

9 TALLEST: Luke Gross, USA – 206cm (Left)

... and Simon Shaw, England – 206cm (right)

10 MOST DROP GOALS: Jonny Wilkinson, England, 8 (below)

World Cup records

Advantage

Ball held up in goal

Collapsing Ruck or Maul

Doctor Needed

Drop out 22

Failure to Bind Properly

Falling over Player

Free Kick

High Tackle

Not Releasing ball

Penalty kick

Punching

Scrum awarded

Stamping

Throw or forward Pass

**Throw in Scrum
Not Straight**

Try and penalty

**Wheeling Scrum 90°
or more**

THE INSIDE TRACK

ALL BLACKS The nickname given to the New Zealand team, coined by British newspaper *The Daily Mail* on the 1905 tour.

BACKS Seven of the 15 players in a team are backs. They don't take part in the scrum or lineouts and often score the majority of the tries.

BACK ROW The openside flanker (number seven), blindside flanker (number six) and No 8 make up the back row of the scrum. The most prolific trio – i.e. the back row that has played together in the most internationals – is the England three of Neil Back, Richard Hill and Lawrence Dallaglio, who were together when they won the World Cup in 2003. The presence of the two flankers is one of the key differences between rugby union and rugby league, which has 13 players in each team.

(OPPOSITE) LAWRENCE DALLAGLIO, ENGLAND'S MOST CAPPED BACK ROW FORWARD

BARBARIANS A legendary invitation side which played its first game in 1880, inspired by William Percy Carpmael. Also called the Baa-Baas, they have enjoyed some epic matches down the years, playing all the major club teams and international sides in their famous black and white hoops.

BLINDSIDE FLANKER This player wears number six and he packs down on the blind (or short side) of the scrum. Great exponents include New Zealand's Michael Jones (who was in Rugby World's Team of the Millennium) and England's Richard Hill. Will be expected to put in a huge number of tackles.

CALCUTTA CUP Contested in all matches between England and Scotland, it was made – in the 1870s – from melted down rupees left over when the Calcutta Rugby Club was disbanded.

(RIGHT) SCOTLAND WON THE CALCUTTA CUP IN 2006: CAPTAIN JASON WHITE ACCEPTING THE TROPHY

CENTRE Every great side will have an inside centre (No 12) and an outside centre (No 13) working in perfect harmony. The inside is often the distributor or creator while the outside should be a little quicker. A good inside centre should also be a good kicker out of hand, working with the outside-half. The outside centre needs expert handling and the eye for a gap.

CONVERSION A kick taken after a try and worth two points if the ball is sent over the crossbar.

FORWARDS The eight men entrusted with the prime job of winning the ball. They form the scrum and lineout and will often be around in the rucks and mauls, battling with the opposition.

FULL-BACK The last line of defence, the full-back wears No 15. In the modern game he needs to be as adept in attack as in defence and a reliable kicker out of hand.

GARRYOWEN A high kick, designed to put huge pressure on the opposition, and named after the famous Irish club. Also known as an up and under.

GRAND SLAM A title contested in the Six Nations Championship. A side is said to have completed a Grand Slam when they beat all other five sides in the Championship, but no trophy is awarded. Wales did a Grand Slam in 2005.

GUINNESS PREMIERSHIP The leading competition in England, the Guinness Premiership is made up of the top 12 teams in the country. Sale Sharks were the champions in 2006. The top four sides in the Guinness Premiership go into a play-off with the final at Twickenham to decide the champions. It was called the Courage League from 1987 to 1997, followed by the Allied Dunbar Premiership and Zurich Premiership, until Guinness took over the sponsorship for the 2005-06 season. Leicester won four successive titles from 1999 to 2003.

HAKA The name given to the war dance or ritual carried out by a number of teams in the rugby world, before a game starts, most notably used by the New Zealand All Blacks. It is used to throw down a challenge to the opposition and is a popular part of the modern game.

HEINEKEN CUP Europe's premier competition, the best sides from England, Ireland, Scotland, Wales, France and Italy contest the Heineken Cup each season. It kicked off in 1996, when it was won by Toulouse. Leicester were the first side to retain the trophy, winning it 15–9 against Munster in 2002.

HOME NATIONS England, Ireland, Scotland and Wales.

HOOKER Standing in the middle of the front row of the scrum, the hooker needs to strong enough to pack down, while he is expected to be a devastating presence around the field and he also throws into the lineout. When there is a scrum they have to 'hook' the ball back when it is fed in by the scrum-half.

IRB The International Rugby Board, the world governing body of the game of rugby union.

(ABOVE) THE LINEOUT HAS BECOME A CRUCIAL PART OF THE GAME

LINEOUT The set piece staged when the ball is kicked out of play. The hooker throws the ball in and the attacking side decides how many players are in the lineout. Anything from four to eight is normal.

MAGNERS LEAGUE The new name for the Celtic League, contested in the UK and Ireland between the best sides in Wales, Scotland and Ireland.

MAUL A ruck when the ball is kept up in the air. A massive battle for the ball with one side trying to march the ball up the field, the other using brute force to stop it.

22-METRE LINE With the rise of the metric system the 20-yard line was abolished. Rugby's equivalent of football's penalty box. If the defensive team kicks the ball in their own 22 the lineout is taken where the ball crosses the line. If they kick it out, from outside their own 22 (except if after a penalty is awarded) the lineout is taken from where they kicked the ball.

OUTSIDE-HALF Rugby's quarterback, the outside-half is the pivot for any team, setting up the back moves. Usually the goalkicker as well, Jonny Wilkinson showed how valuable a great outside-half is in the 2003 World Cup, winning the tournament deep into extra time with a drop goal.

PENALTY Awarded for a number of offences, a side winning a penalty can decide to kick at goal and if the ball is sent through the posts and over the upright it is worth three points.

PROP
Loosehead The loosehead (or number one) props on the left hand side of the scrum, next to where the scrum-half puts the ball into the scrum. One of the unsung heroes, they need huge upper-body strength.
Tighthead The tighthead (or number three) props on the right hand side of the scrum, they are the pillar of strength on which all great packs prosper. Some coaches say when selecting a side you should "pick the tighthead, pick the goalkicker and then pick 13 players to take the field with them" so important is the tighthead to a side.

PROVINCES In Ireland four provinces – Ulster, Munster, Leinster and Connacht – were formed to cover Ireland, both north and south. In the modern game the Irish team is picked from these provinces. In Ireland club sides form the tier below provinces, feeding their players into them.

(BELOW) MUNSTER, THE MEN IN RED, LIFTED THE HEINEKEN CUP IN 2006

RUCK A ruck occurs when the ball is on the ground, normally after a player is tackled. It is formed when two players on their feet, one from each team, arrive at the ball. The referee will often shout 'ruck' to the players when it has been formed as they can no longer put their hands on the ball.

SCRUM-HALF The link between the forwards and the backs, the scrum-half (number nine) needs to be a great passer, organiser, runner and defender, possessing great all-round skills. George Gregan is the most prolific scrum-half in the history of the game, overtaking Jason Leonard's previous record for caps won, in 2005.

SECOND ROW Also referred to as locks, these guys wear four and five and have the key responsibility of winning ball in the lineout. They will be the tallest player on the field, but since the game turned professional they are required to do far more than win lineout ball. Many act as a fourth or fifth back rower, marauding around the field and some like John Eales and Allan Martin have even been known to kick a few goals.

SIN BIN A player who transgresses certain laws is sent to the sin bin for 10 minutes, once the referee has shown the yellow card. The first player to be sent to the sin bin in the World Cup was Manuel Contepomi in 2003.

SIX NATIONS CHAMPIONSHIP The annual competition staged between the test sides of England, Scotland, Wales, Ireland, France and Italy. Won by France in 2006. It was changed from the Five Nations to Six in 2000 when Italy joined.

SPRINGBOKS The nickname given to the South Africa team

SUPER 14 The premier competition in the southern hemisphere, it features the 14 biggest sides (non-international) in New Zealand, South Africa and Australia. It was won by New Zealand's Crusaders (from Canterbury) in 2006 when it was transformed from a Super 12 into a Super 14, two new teams joining the competition. Each side plays 13 games with the top four going into a play-off competition. It was founded in 1996 after rugby turned professional. There are five sides from New Zealand, five from South Africa, with four from Australia in the Super 14. The Auckland Blues won the first two titles.

TRIPLE CROWN In the Six Nations any home nation (Ireland, Wales, Scotland and England) beating all three others is awarded the Triple Crown. Won in 2006 by the Irish.

(ABOVE) IRELAND CAPTAIN BRIAN O'DRISCOLL PROUDLY SHOWS OFF THE 2006 TRIPLE CROWN TROPHY

TRI-NATIONS The annual battle of the three giants of the southern hemisphere; New Zealand, Australia and South Africa, the Tri-Nations kicked off in 1996 after the game turned professional. Dominated in recent years by New Zealand, they won all but one title from 2002 to 2006.

TRY The grounding of the ball over the try line earns five points. Unlike in

(ABOVE) SIMPLY THE BEST ...
DAISUKE OHATA, JAPAN'S RECORD BREAKING WING

American football the player in possession must put the ball down and must be in control when he does so.

WALLABIES The nickname given to the Australia team.

WING The quickest players on the field, the right and left wing are the players who score the most tries. It is crucial that a world-class wing is as

good in defence as attack. The leading scorer in Test history is Japan's Daisuke Ohata, who went past David Campese's previous record in 2006.

WOODEN SPOON The title given to the side that finishes bottom of the Six Nations Championship. After England finished bottom in 1983 the Wooden Spoon Charity was formed and since then it has raised millions of pounds supporting mentally, physically and socially disadvantaged children and young people.

Picture credits

This is a Parragon Book

This edition first published in 2007

Parragon Books Ltd
Queen Street House
4 Queen Street
Bath BA1 1HE, UK

ISBN 978-1-4054-9936-1

This edition created by Endeavour London Limited

Text: Paul Morgan
Design: Paul Welti
Picture research: Paul Morgan
Edited by: Mark Fletcher
Project management: Mary Osborne

Printed in China